THE FLAME OF TRANSFORMATION TURNS TO LIGHT

(NINETY-NINE GHAZALS WRITTEN IN ENGLISH)

THE FLAME OF
TRANSFORMATION
TURNS TO LIGHT

Ninety-Nine Ghazals Written in English

May 2 – August 2, 2002

Daniel Abdal-Hayy Moore

The Ecstatic Exchange

2007

PHILADELPHIA

For quotes any longer than those for critical articles and reviews,
contact:
The Ecstatic Exchange,
6470 Morris Park Road, Philadelphia, PA 19151-2403
email: abdalhayy@danielmoorepoetry.com

First Edition
ISBN: 978-0-6151-4273-9
Published by *The Ecstatic Exchange,*
6470 Morris Park Road, Philadelphia, PA 19151-2403

Cover and text design by Abdallateef Whiteman / www.cwdm.co.uk
Cover collage by the author
Back cover photograph by Malika Moore

بسم

To all those most generous hosts in Turkey
my first journey there
and to
Faruk Dilaver, sweet sohbets from the akhira,
and
Shaykh ibn al-Habib
(and the continuation of the Habibiyya)
Shaykh Bawa Muhaiyuddeen
and
Baji Tayyaba Khanum

❖

The earth is not bereft
of Light

CONTENTS

PART 2

THE FLAME OF TRANSFORMATION
TURNS TO LIGHT

AUTHOR'S INTRODUCTION

I AM NOT, by nature, a formalist. Stubbornness, ignorance, arrogance, rebellion, whatever it is has more or less curtailed my writing of poems in formal structures, in spite of the sonnet sequences in *Ramadan Sonnets* of 1986, though most of them are free verse poems, or poems in open form, which I defend by reminding us that "sonnet" really means "little song."

But on my first visit to Turkey in 2002, in the company of heartfelt travelers, I took with me on the airplane the downloaded "rules" of writing poems in *ghazal* form, reading them while up in the air, and then writing the first one of this present collection, which takes place where it really did take place – up in the air!

In an entry by Akhilesh Mithal on the website, *Frontline,* we have the following history of the form: "In Arabic, *"ghazal"* means a lover talking to his beloved amorously. The ghazal was developed further and to its maximum potential in Iran and in India where Persian was the court language of the Turcomans, Afghans and the Mughals who ruled in the North and the Bahamanis and their successors in the South. Of the Persian poets, Hafiz of Shiraz enjoys the highest reputation. The Indian poets held in esteem for Persian verse are Amir Khusrau (13th century) and Mirza Bedil (18th century). Khusrau also wrote in Hindi and was devoted to the great Sufi Nizamuddin Auliya. Khusrau's Persian and Hindi verse is sung at Sufi shrines even today, some seven centuries later. On the anniversary of the saint's death, the Urs festivities start with *qawwals* singing a Khusrau verse."

The form, for ghazal formalists at least, is rather strict, though also rather simple, and works best in the languages of its origin, Arabic, Farsi, Urdu, Bengali, etc., where there are more rhyme words because of similar vowel endings than we have in English. The poem is made up of couplets, and after the first in which the end word is identical but the penultimate words are two words that rhyme, the following couplets have a first line that is unrhymed in its ending, and the second line with a new penultimate rhyme word chiming with those two in the first couplet, and then the identical final word repeated for all the succeeding couplets to the end. This is the strict interpretation of the rhyme scheme. (For the fastidious formalist in the ghazal tradition, I should note that I made one minor technical error in the first poems, especially in Turkey, in my understanding of the rules, by in the first couplet repeating the next to last rhyme word before the identical end-word. I somehow thought it was the same word repeated twice. I have often remedied this in editing these poems for the present volume.)

The other characteristics of traditional ghazals are a "ravishing disunity" (to use Agha Shahid Ali's phrase) between the couplets, treating each couplet as a non-discursive thread, each one like a unique string of lustrous pearls by itself, only obliquely connected to the other couplets in the poem. Leaps and glitters, even disruptions and seeming distractions of the poet, are prized, though in the best poems there is an underlying unity indicating a world so vast in spiritual as well as physical terms, that we can barely contain it in either consciousness or language.

The other aspect is that the poet "signs" his or her name in the final couplet, by inserting it somehow into the flow, even addressing oneself directly in chiding, admonishing, or even praising terms. I was given the name *Ameen* (Trustworthy) in the desert of Algeria in the late 70s by a blind wali, Shaykh Isa of Laghouat (may Allah be pleased with him), though I have rarely used it. But I decided to sign these poems with it since it can also be flexibly utilized in its familiar meaning of *Amen.*

I took to the form with enthusiasm, and newly trained my usual approach for inspired composition to stick by the form with little variation (modern practitioners in English take many liberties with it and still call them ghazals). But I also wanted poems that responded to my daily thought and experience, both light and serious, in natural speech flow, even in the more metaphysical flights.

What I ended up with was a kind of travelogue through a physical and spiritual Turkey, visiting Rumi in his tomb in Konya, whose spirit stayed with me for a long time afterward, and various other saints, including their "national" poet, wild and wandering dervish, Yunus Emre. And then when I returned to America, I continued writing ghazals until I had a total of ninety-nine. At that point I felt the old restlessness against formalist constraints, and had to actually wrench myself out of writing ghazals to get back to my own internal sense of open form by which I wrote and continue to write my poems.

For although holding to a strict form shapes the inspiration and constrains it, and it may do so both memorably and magically, it also hampers certain intuitive leaps by its priority requirements. Ultimately I'll leave such formality to its better practitioners with all my blessings, and carry on striving for the perfection of that more elusive poem whose traces are harder to come by perhaps but for me at least, lead, God willing, to a more open space.

Yet for a time, and actually much longer than I anticipated, I enjoyed the rubric's cube of the ghazal form in which to breathe out these wispy or chunky inspirations, the garden edges held tightly together (more or less) by a tradition which I salute, imperfectly but gratefully, in these poems.

All things are concealed in all. One of them all is the concealer of the rest – their corporeal vessel, external, visible and movable.

— PARACELSUS, *The Coelum Philosphorum*

In the ash that remains at the bottom of the grave, there lies the king's diadem.

— *Livre de Arthéphius,*
Bibliothèque des Philosophes Chimiques, Paris, 1741

One time when the Shaikh came to Tus, the people entreated him to speak before an assembly. The Shaikh consented. At dawn a platform was set up in the Kanaqah of the Master and people began arriving and seating themselves. When the Shaikh came forth, the chanters recited from the Qor'an. Meanwhile so many people had come in that there was no room left. The master of ceremonies rose to his feet and said: "May God have mercy on each person who takes one step forward from where he is." The Shaikh exclaimed: "God bless Mohammad and his family, one and all!" And the Shaikh drew his hand down over his face and said: "Everything I wished to say and everything the prophets declared, he has just said: 'May you advance one step from what you are.'" And the Shaikh didn't say another word but came down from the platform and with that he brought the assembly to a close.

MOHAMMED EBN-E MONAVVAR,
The Secrets of God's Mystical Oneness

PART I

TURKEY

1 UP IN THE AIR ON OUR WAY TO TURKEY

We're up in the air on our way to Turkey flying at night –
It's eerie to think we're in this tiny dot in space flying at night

So many people crammed and belted in their seats trying to sleep
Uncomfortably tossing and turning to and fro sighing at night

If we really knew how to fly we wouldn't need airplanes at all
But would go where our hearts' prayers wished multiplying at night

Shafts of space so brilliant they'd dazzle the distant stars
With illuminations pouring through our blood denying the night

Doubts and hesitations all but vanished away completely
As well as uncontrollable weeping by day and crying by night

A giant door open in space where mirroring rivers of energy flow
God creates antimatter and matter with – even supplying the night

There beyond every human emotion and elegant characteristic
Our plane wants to sail in perfect splendor indemnifying the night

Never to come back in quite the same state as the one departed in
But alchemically transformed – sweetly but firmly calcifying the night

Seeing God's Face directly in every mortally soulful manifestation
From here to eternity victoriously vying with night –

Are thoughts like these passing through anyone else's head
In this throbbing metal angel en route to Turkey flying at night ?

These thoughts of one tiny passenger fitfully unable to sleep –
Ameen – probing with feeble cardiac flashlight spying at night!

5/2

2 THE BELOVED'S BRIDE

I've seen the Beloved's Bride stand up in a white ocean
And everything suddenly turn from waves to a white ocean

If you saw her smile even once you'd fall in a deep swoon –
If you caught her moonlike glance you'd drown in deep insight's ocean

She who has given herself over wholeheartedly to love
So that her face has become a moon that intensely ignites oceans

Boats drift from her hair – wrecks sink like stones with all hands –
No one drowning in adoration ever fights oceans

In her heart everything transforms from minute to monumental –
Nothing goes unaccounted for even in black-as-night oceans

Her heart has become a living locus where all the world's oceans meet
And unite in surf-breaking *al-hamdulillahs* of delight oceans

Birds don't fly over her head – so lit with love is she –
Her force field rising high in the sky from her light ocean

She loves so deeply that she's become love itself
Charging the air so electrically it excites oceans

A Bride who's become so pure in the intensity of her love
Waves themselves say *Ameen* on her eternal wedding-night's ocean

5/3

3   HER DREAM OF MEHMET

"Wake up!" Cried Mehmet waking her up in a clear dream
She woke up hearing his voice calling out in her ear's dream

"I want to go with you to visit Sa'bân-i Veli's tomb today
But you'll need a coat to keep warm on the bus – O dear dream

It may get cold on your way to your final sweet destination
Though all of our life on earth – it's true – is a mere dream"

She woke up having heard Mehmet's spectral voice wafting
And ran to her closet in this world's shadowy frontier dream

And found a red coat on a hanger she'd forgotten was there –
With some chocolates in a pocket since it was not a severe dream

Then on the bus just now to visit Sa'bân-i Veli's tomb and tekke –
Driving through mountainous landscapes melting into her seer's dream –

When saintly Faruk Abi heard of her dream and the coat and the sweets
He produced chocolates for everyone making *this world* appear dream!

So *alhamdulillah* at the beginning and *ameen* at the end
On this journey that passes through such a sincere dream

5/4

4 THE MOON

The moon beams out across the ocean in a path of perfect radiance
Its white light coring a disk in the sky already bedecked with radiance

Each wave crest reflects that spotlight an infinite number of times
But each one mirrors the whole moon too if you inspect the radiance

Like rolling palaces filled with light each bright crest sparkles
Yet the moon stays fixed in the sky alone with its correct radiance

It's the cold moon reflecting the light of the hot sun of Unity
Like a goblet filled with a heady wine as if to inject radiance

Is the sun so far away the moon can't physically catch its light?
A dead celestial body in space whose surface collects radiance?

Prophet Muhammad's face – they said – was like the full moon of Badr
Where in the hearts of the warriors of Truth you could detect radiance

His heart – peace be upon him – was marriage of sun and moon together
And though the sun be far off the moon's close enough to connect radiance

This light of his love bubbles up through the single ocean of our hearts
Born in physical bodies in this life in order to reflect radiance

O what a moon song to be sung out loud here in Turkey's moon-land
By *Ameen* – son of the moon – may he be shipwrecked *in* radiance!

5/4

5 SA'BÂN-i VELI'S TOMB IN KASTAMONU

We return from a visit to Sa'bân-i Veli who left his perfumed remains
    behind
But as we said farewell did we also tell our self to remain behind?

As we pressed our faces close to the grille to greet the saint
Did we let his tomb in Paradise keep our feelings of loss and gain behind?

We crossed high mountains of fir trees and banks of snow
To drink at his *zam-zam* fountain and leave both joy and pain behind

Was that his face at the window – was that his cat slinking by?
We felt his glance telling us to leave all disdain behind

As we drove through the night back from our visit
The day that started sunny and bright left a fine curtain of rain behind

What sweet relief to be able to visit such a one
Knowing that through the veil of this world there lies such a saint behind

O self of *Ameen* and of everyone else of God's lovers
Walk into the saint's presence and leave all need to explain behind!

5/4

6   THE BIRDS OF ANKARA

The birds of Ankara greet the dawn filling the trees
Their shrill song without trumpets piccolos or flutes is filling the trees

They woke me up for the prayer with first morning light
Its patchwork of dervish-bright mist already spilling through trees

They insist on beauty – these birds – they sing out to make it catch fire
It's so incandescent if their song were flames it'd be killing the trees

They've just arrived from God's tall poplars in the Unseen
Putting on the feathers of this world like zeros nilling the trees

Their chorus is so exalted – like calliopes from heaven
Scattering sweet drops of Truth like teachers instilling the trees

Suddenly with sunrise the birds calm down to single note-sizzles
Chatting from bird to bird as if windowsilling the trees

God sent these birds – their song – the dawn – the Messenger – the prayer
And lifted this world into full view willing the trees

Ameen is all we can say to it – its prayer is so strong –
Now daylight is bringing its tarnished silvers chilling the trees

5/5

7   ROSES FLOATING ON THE OCEAN

(written upon entering the tomb of Ahmed Dede in Ankara)

We're roses floating across on the wide ocean's waves
Broken stems from a bush that grows by the side of the ocean's
waves

Our rose stems have been torn from the bush
But we long to return with the elixir of Unity by its powerful potion's
waves

Some stems are broken at a harsh angle – some jaggedly cut
Yet none can be healed by this world's so-called soothing lotion's waves

O how far must we travel before we reach the beginning again?
Leaving behind once and for all our destructive emotions' waves?

His divine rosebush of origin grows in a nearby Secret Garden
Whose iron gate opens at a single touch of love's motion's waves

Petal by petal and stem by stem we are restored
And return to our original stillness beyond all our life's commotion's
waves

Each petal of the heart beating for Allah alone
Brings us closer to the central rosebush of our heart's locomotion's waves

Ameen says "Place each broken petal back on the bush
By the intoxicating smell alone of God's rose – and never shun its waves"

5/5

8 AHMED DEDE'S GREETING

Ahmed Dede himself gave me the poem of the rose in his tomb today –
He didn't greet me when I entered but I greeted him at his tomb today

Then as I sat among the lovers singing love's sweet songs
And saw each of us as roses floating on an ocean lit by the moon today

The inspired thought progressed that we were also like roses
Broken from their rosebush like a bride torn from her groom today

That we long to be reunited to the light of God's rosebush
Like Rumi's reed to its reedbed in this reclining saint's rose-colored room
     today

Then dear friend Musa spoke saying Ahmed Dede greeted *him* his first time
And since he hadn't greeted me I felt a deep sadness lower its boom today

Then Musa went on and said Faruk Abi told him that at that very moment
Ahmed Dede wanted to give Musa a rose that was in full bloom that day

So they went outside and found a rose broken on the ground by its rosebush
And at that my heart leapt completely out of its gloom today

Shouting *Allah!* since Ahmed Dede had greeted me after all by the Rose
    poem –
Ameen slave of Allah – His lover thrown into a happy swoon today

5/6

THE YUNUS EMRE FESTIVAL IN ESKISEHIR

At the Yunus Emre Festival the mosquitos flew in for a tasty feast
Especially at the picnic where we were cornucopia'd with a tasty feast

Scrumptuous baked pastries – fresh lettuce – tomatoes with celestial
  flavor
All of life became opposite to that of a hasty feast

The blessing of Yunus from God's orchards of generosity
Poured from heaven to earth and back again leaving zesty traces of feast

O Yunus – you walked on this ground barefoot and also with shoes on
Knowing with each breath the sweetness of God's lacy feast

Did mosquitos bite you too and did you let them
As you roved this earth as love's troubador at His Majesty's feast?

5/6

10 A VISION OF YUNUS

I see Yunus walking with stallion body and face of a harp through this
      green land
Singing birds on branches and hair like rivers through this green land

A voice like thunder and eyes like lightning as he gambols along
Each ear hearing him attuning itself to the wavelengths of a serene land

His fingers like raindrops touching each leaf and grassblade –
Each pebble and feeler of insect graced with love in this seen land

In the Unseen Land he comes and goes at ease because his heart is filled
      with God –
His wisdom-songs proof of his passage through this soon-to-be-
      smithereens land

5/6

11 GOING TO KONYA

Tomorrow we're getting on a bus in Ankara and going to Konya
Most of my adult life I've wanted to be going to Konya

Will it be raining tiny celestial cities or crescent rainbows like flying
        birds?
Will it be sizzling hot with bronze sunlight or snowing in Konya?

Will Mevlana be tall or short – visible or invisible?
Will he greet me as I enter his tomb – his smile a sweet breeze
        blowing in Konya?

Will there be a giant elephant in a dark house
And will three blind men try to describe it – totally not knowing in
        Konya?

Will the tomb rise up into the starry heavens themselves –
Its turquoise dome entering dimension after dimension – each
        glowing in Konya?

Will a cape of gorgeous feathers from the Great Simurgh fall from the
        ceiling
And float slowly onto Rumi's tomb gracefully flowing in Konya?

Will the Path to Allah open up like the yellow brick road to Oz
And every Lion Scarecrow and Tin Man of our souls be growing
        in Konya?

Am I expecting too much – *O faint heart* – or am I expecting too little?
Will the tomb of Rumi be silent as stone or softly echoing in Konya?

Will I see Rumi face to face at some moment in some way
And forever after my heart be like an open ocean rowing in Konya?

Some saints leave traces – some saints leave majestic mountains –
Rumi's stature with God a whole world seems to be shadowing *from* Konya

When we step off the bus will my feet tingle? Will I hear the hammer
Beating the copper pot Rumi heard – its heart-pulse bestowing on Konya?

Will Shems appear in ragged cloak and fierce sun-scorched face –
Heart like a catapult whole galaxies into infinity throwing in Konya?

Ah *Ameen* – you've waited long enough all your 61 years to now –
Go to sleep and tomorrow *insha'Allah* you'll finally be going to Konya!

5/7

12　IN RUMI'S TOMB IN KONYA

A sky shaped like a face – *no it can't be that*
A wingéd horse on fire in the middle of the air – *no it can't*
　　be that

A sound of bells that burns from the feet to the heart
A whisper of hidden words falling from the top of a tree – *no it can't*
　　be that

A look across centuries that today is enshrouded in the world
The touch of a child's hand who already knows the secret – *no it can't*
　　be that

A bridge of light in all the usual places
A bird that expands to embrace every living heart – *no it can't be that*

An eye that beholds the cave where the Prophet became Messenger
A sing-song voice speaking perfect rhyming sentences – *no it can't be that*

Hello before you arrive and Hello again before you get up to go
A kiss across green water that reflects both sun and moon – *no it can't*
　　be that

A call from within Rumi's shirt so old its threads look like rain
A light that slides up a corner of the tomb and fills the body – *no it can't*
　　be that

What is it then? Is there any answer?
Is it possible to say? – *no it can't be that*

Ameen was gone for a moment but something remained
There's only a trace left in the air from all of us – *no it can't be that*

Mevlana – we certainly had a magnificent celebration
Does it need to end? – no – please – *it can't be that*

5/7
(*at Rumi's tekke in Konya*)

13 LIFE IS A MYSTERY TILL THE VERY END

There's no question but that our life is a mystery till the very end
We're born and must feed off the earth our mother till the very end

A restless two-year old boy on the bus back from Konya makes me
    think –
What causes his restlessness – and how will its flurry end?

Sometimes he's silent – sometimes he whimpers and cries –
Will it just be tucked in his bed that will bring him a merry end?

The jittery night-lights of the world flashing by in a rush –
This world or the next – day or night – life or death – when will contraries
    end?

Restless until we gain complete fulfillment at last –
Reaching the tree and sucking the juice from a cherry's end

Like the little boy facing forward into the night on his mother's lap –
Why do we think the end of this life has only a scary end?

Bright eyes – little fists – pacifier firmly entrenched – now he's finally
    quiet –
Ameen – you've just been scratching your overly busy head – your
    hairy end!

5/7

14 STILL THERE

O sweet Mevlana – I woke up this morning and you were still there –
The clock from Saʾbân-i Veli ticking – birds singing – and you were still
    there

I saw a white horse standing alone in a meadow waiting for you
And a waterfall of most delicious clear water beginning to spill there

The desert is a place where many pack animals tread
But their traces are lost in the sand when night falls with its chill there

I think you are serving us trays of sweetmeats – O my beloved –
To give out to people assembled following God's will there

I should expect a great golden bird to appear at the window
And close its wings and sing honeyed notes as it sits on the sill there

How do you come so close – dear Mevlana – so far from Konya?
Somehow you never left me – but I didn't know it until I was filled there

We've got a few million miles left to travel in this world – dear heart –
But it's easier now with you helping to turn the mill there

The leaves of each tree have a city on them in fiery conflagration
But the water of love may put out the fires if we carry it uphill there

At last – dear one – my heart can hear its deep murmurings
And the ocean as it branches with its widely rivering rills there

Shaykh Muhammad Habib – Bawa – Ahmed Dede – the living guides –
Have white horses in the meadow so green with sweet chlorophyll there

I must go back to sleep for a moment Mevlana – but don't leave me –
As *Ameen* floats out across a lake that lies so tranquil and still there

5/8

15 GREAT REWARD

There's no point going on a journey and not expecting a great reward
Then a moment may come that will clearly display a great reward

The face of a child – the way a bird lands folding its wings in a tree –
A glance or word poured from the heart – all may indicate reward

It's hard to go back to sleep once the tap's been turned on
And the flow of meanings pours out to relate reward

One step after another in this world – or even making a run for it –
But once you set out you must yearningly hope for no late reward

Ameen – if you set your face to the Ka'ba each moment – each breath
You won't even be able to calculate reward

5/8

16   ON A BUS TO ANTALYA

Now we're on an impossibly huge streamlined bus heading to Antalya
We're gliding along the highway at night heading to Antalya

It's an eight and a half hour's journey and we left at midnight
Not knowing what to expect there – it could be a *beheading* in
　　　Antalya!

We just passed three men (2:30AM) on motorbikes by the side of the
　　　road –
We on a ship on wheels like the Titanic – asphalt wave-treading to
　　　Antalya

We're going to a very luxurious Fantasy *Naturland* Resort in Kemer –
Saunas and forest walks and massages – we won't be *underfed* in
　　　Antalya

But somehow I feel that after all our other experiences (*Rumi and
　　　Yunus*)
We'll be walking up golden stairways through gossamer netting in
　　　Antalya

A taste of spiritual nectar given to us on silver spoons
By a master of *all-but-Allah-forgetting* in Antalya

Ameen can't sleep on this monstrous bus at 2:45AM –
Thinking also of some really comfortable bedding in Antalya!

5/9

17 HALLELUJAH!

If snow-capped peaks and lush green vales could speak they'd sing *Glory*
    Hallelujah!
Though they can't shoulder God's trust as man does – they'd sing *Glory*
    Hallelujah!

God wrapped the road to Antalya in jaggedly high mountains
Of rugged shale and pale chalky green as earth's fastenings – *Glory*
    Hallelujah!

The crescent moon in a sunrise sky streaked with ribbons of red –
The stillness and vastness of everything – *Glory Hallelujah!*

Vista after vista – I'm in the front seat of the bus facing a picture window –
Gorgeous green and brick red rocky panoramas that keep opening – *Glory*
    Hallelujah!

There's a mountain over there that looks like *Jabal Nur*
Silhouetted against the powder blue sky of early morning – *Glory Hallelujah!*

You could almost say God didn't know quite where to begin
So in an instant He poured majestic beauty over everything – *Glory*
    Hallelujah!

What are eyes for but to see God's Beauty? What's a heart for but to
Love His Majesty – as He makes the earth come alive springing – *Glory*
    Hallelujah!

(As I scribble this poem rumbling along I swear we passed a mosque
just now
With a sign in lights strung between twin minarets writing: *Laila
Hallelujah!*)

Perched in the air like this in total awe at what's before me –
Ameen is the last whisper before there is nothing – *Glory Hallelujah!*

5/9

18   NO SLEEP BUT WAKING UP

I didn't think I was getting any sleep on the bus
But then I would suddenly wake up

Red poppies along the highway to Antalya
Like the field to Oz where Dorothy tried to suddenly wake up

I think in spite of the fantasy nature of this place
The point here is that we're meant to suddenly wake up

Though of course we don't think we're actually asleep
We'll know it's true when we suddenly wake up

The heart is a light by the light of Allah —
When the light is switched on we suddenly wake up

Life is too short to sleep forever *Ameen* —
The Prophet said when we die we will certainly *suddenly* wake up

5/9

19 EVERYTHING'S IN A WHIRL

Everything's in a whirl – the saucers and cups are dancing together
      tonight –
Even the stars are bending to listen – learning to sing in harmony
      together tonight

There exists an old cobbler – his shoes are so special –
The wearers of them never touch ground – even though they're made of
      leather – tonight

All kinds of animals from primeval forests are on the prowl –
All kinds of birds are flying in from faraway – preening a special feather
      tonight

If you say it's one thing it's not – if silent speak – if speaking stay silent
Whatever it is you hold onto – it's time to sever tonight

Is Allah far or near? What about the jugular?
All threads and disparaties are going to get gathered together tonight

Ah – a star is rising – a particular star—a green star of prophetic light
Ameen – be there for its scattering drops to fall in abundant measure
      tonight

5/9

20 THE MAN WHO WALKED AT THE EDGE

There once was a man with a face of gold light who walked at the edge
He spoke of things nobody understood – since he always walked at the edge

His eyes often lost their specific look of belonging to him –
Words seemed to come from another dimension when he talked at the edge

His body got dirty – his body needed food – as do we all –
but like putting a garment on or off – sublime indifference stalked at his edge

He comes among us with no foul smoke hanging anywhere near him –
At moments of pure light any taint gets balked at the edge

Ameen – let your love flow just as purely in every direction
And you'll soon see how this perfect no-one walks at the edge

5/9

21 SOHBET WITH MEVLANA

I'm having *sohbet* with Mevlana and he won't let me go
But I don't really want to – I could stay here forever

Like being held in a box of whispering light
This place of bright sky could banish fear forever

Even sounds become music like the quail outside calling –
All space is transversed in the innermost ear forever

Children yell out in Turkish as they run along the trails
Delivering messages from heaven to be held dear forever

Take this sweet – this halva steaming with light —
In the air is a rose-scent that brings cheer forever

If I get up to go he'll come with me I know –
To get lost together in a single tear forever

Mevlana – invisible messenger of my heart –
I want to say *Ameen* and then remain near forever

5/9

22 ABANDONMENT AND SHAME

They left without me – childhood feelings – abandonment and shame –
Why left behind while they went on – to my abandonment and shame?

Life's beginning is isolation – life's end is the very same
The world goes on without us – to our abandonment and shame

All our actions perform circus stunts repeatedly in the game –
But hearts stand naked on Judgment Day of abandonment and shame

Nothing we've done put us here – no act will blow out the flame –
It's a hard thing to understand the essence of abandonment and shame

God's Unique and forms us unique – the way He's fashioned our frame –
Then places souls within us who feel abandonment and shame

Abandonment – unable by ourselves to fulfill His Divine Names –
But that we're *anything* apart from Him is *true* cause for shame

I felt left all alone while others somewhere were enjoying their fame
So I entered another dimension foreign to abandonment and shame

Is this one you see today he who goes round with my name?
Ameen – press grateful and forgiving lips on abandonment and shame

5/9

23 MEVLANA AND I TOOK A WALK

Mevlana and I took a walk today but he kept me to himself –
A cat on the path purred when I touched him and kept me to himself

Otherwise trees and statues and birds and strangers
And everyone else I saw seemed strangely bereft of himself

So I came back to the room with you – Mevlana – without food or
        drink –
Shall we eat the food and drink Allah has kept to Himself?

I can't see the tray but I can smell the rose-scent wafting from the dish
Of the fish that stood up in Moses' basket and leapt to Himself

Is this the fountain of Eternal Life then that we drink from the air?
If I breathe it in in small sips will it just be theft from Himself?

Each moment changes through its own spectrum according to God's
        Names
But isn't the drink we drink each moment breath from Himself?

Then there's death to contend with – for each one of us in the middle
        of life –
But – *Ameen* – that's the secret drink we can't drink that He's kept to
        Himself

5/9

24 THE WINDOW OF MY ROOM

Mediterranean fish-stink drifts through the window of my room –
I expect Mevlana to take visible shape and drift through the window of my
    room

I want epic grandeur in the rhymes of these *ghazals* – mountains and deserts –
Red skies full of light – displayed like a gift through the window of my
    room

It's morning now as I continue this poem and light begins to rise – bird-
    skittle
Machinery noise radio static human speech – now uplift through the
    window of my room

As the world advances through its frivolous phases the Beloved seems aloof –
The exchange between form and meaning seems to shift through the
    window of my room

Would that every moment we could see this as Allah's delicious revelation
    and say *Ameen* –
Everything resolved into One – *O Divine Thrift!* – through the window of
    my room!

5/10

25 THE ECSTASY OF THE MOMENT

The ecstasy of the moment is a star-burst vase full of blue clouds –
Flaming flowers bloom in stems that billow from a vase full of blue
clouds

"Where have you been?" God asks – but the reply is always *"With you!"* –
Even though we might not know it – our true place is in blue clouds

Arriving with heavy luggage – we can leave it all at His door –
All the worth in this world is nothing but mad races of blue clouds

Have I heard even one word of truth and believed it?
Is my heart in my body – or are all its beatings laced in blue clouds?

There is no one speaking when Yunus Emre opens his mouth
But only the creative Source of the grace of blue clouds

On tables spread out at dawn for the feast of this world
God's Generous Abundance is served on plates of blue clouds

It's always the opening celestial flower of the moment we seek
When the listening-most part of our heart is chased by blue clouds

Ameen – this life's all misty pictures hiding meanings within meanings
of light –
So set your heartbeats and footsteps to match the pace of blue clouds

5/10

26   THE PROPHET NOAH

This Turkish resort has giant cement animals and a concrete Ark of Noah –
Is it the end of the world – animals turned to stone on a concrete Ark of
Noah?

A pair of green octopuses writhing round the concrete bow of the boat –
Two of everything – the usual pairs ready to stomp feet on the Ark of Noah

Noah was a unique prophet told to build a boat in the middle of a desert –
All the better to hear the command Allah had to repeat for the Ark of Noah

Who could imagine a flood in a desert – hot sun mercilessly baking?
But he started plank by plank and nail by nail to build that sweet Ark of
Noah

He'd save what Allah wanted saved – but couldn't save his own son
Who climbed a mountain thinking waters would defeat the Ark of Noah

"Come aboard my son!" – *"No father"* – then Allah finally said to Noah
"He is not of your family" – even the son had no guaranteed seat on the Ark
of Noah

What must it have been for him as prophet and father to be so all alone?
Going by only what Allah said to his heart to complete the Ark of Noah!

Those floodwaters that carried all the animals and the blesséd family of
Noah –
Was it his heart with Truth's harsh waves that beat against the Ark of Noah?

And when it cleared and the waters receded and they reached dry land –
Earth was empty of all except what was dualistically replete on the
        Ark of Noah

God made him crazy – with love and God's wisdom – on an earth gone
        sour –
Only a few were ferried away from Iblis – that low cheat – on the Ark
        of Noah

Ameen – the time seems almost centuries later to have come round
        again –
Calling us to get on board a spiritual *just-down-the-street* Ark of Noah

Floodwaters way over our heads and cities nearly disappeared altogether –
Our guide yells out to us to climb aboard the super fleet Ark of Noah

                                                                5/10

27 THE MELANCHOLY OF OUR DAILY EXISTENCE

There's joy in the air and melancholy in our daily existence –
Worldly hard-edged things keep us in the melancholy of our daily existence

In a cave somewhere a Lament for our lost unity is bent over weeping –
Her hair falls like a waterfall in curls over the melancholy of our daily
     existence

A flute player somewhere is stopping the holes of his reed sounding sad
     notes
As he sits in the harsh dusty daylight of the melancholy of our daily
     existence

An elephant stands by itself somewhere just swaying back and forth
Blowing air out its curling trunk in the melancholy of our daily existence

We get up like soldiers of love from sleep's trenches with our hearts burning –
Even you *Ameen* – momentarily flattened by the melancholy of our daily
     existence

5/11

28 RUINS

Now we're in a tour bus in Antalya going to see ruins –
Phrygian – Hittite – Greek – Roman – we're off to see ruins

A few pillars or basalt bases of pillars propped at angles –
Faces of statues half shorn off – once glorious – now completely in ruins

The Prophet said when passing through ruins we should weep
For those who have passed before and for our selves – soon to *be* ruins

Then there are those who are fearful of mortal annihilation
Who – facing the dust of our days – might be tempted to flee ruins

O Allah – You alone have real existence –
Everything else either rising into life or collapsing unhappily in ruins

In the amphitheater in *Side* Musa recited from Julius Caesar
Marc Anthony's speech after Caesar said "*Et tu* – what me? *Ruins!*"

Ameen – here comes another opportunity to leave your dust self behind –
And your heart to explode into pure light – flying free of ruins

5/11

29 WATERFALL IN PARADISE

There's nothing quite as beautiful as a waterfall in Paradise
Especially when an enlightened guide takes you – *nafs* and all – to Paradise

We walked on bridges over waters gushing gorgeously down rocks
Each sound in God's nature emitting by its essence a clear call to Paradise

Human beings with failings and foibles – toothaches and heartaches –
Connecting us to our original parents and their fall from Paradise

These sparkling – roaring – crashing waters pouring from above
Yelling the word *"love!"* a trillion ways from somewhere tall in Paradise

Where does such power come from? Allah's Beauty and Majesty –
Each thundering waterdrop as if hammered out in some hall in Paradise

The task of our guide – to open hearts wide and free-flowing as waterfalls
Where there is no more trace of worldly or otherworldly quarrel in Paradise

Ameen – you've seen the waters and heard in your heart the full rush of His
      Names –
Now make a run for it and vault over the non-existent wall to Paradise

5/12

30 GIFT OF A ROSE

I want a rose of rich burgundy to give the Mevlevi shopkeeper we met
        today –
You might travel for miles and not meet the like of the young
        shopkeeper we met today

The mountains are high – the sea is low – white clouds float across blue
        expanse –
But a heart full of light in a human being with tears in his eyes is the best
        thing yet today

His face was already open – his lean body tingling with life –
And as we bought a shirt from him in his shop there was a deep
        tête-a-tête today

May his heart be showered with roses – each wise color in love's
        spectrum –
When he saw my talisman necklace his arm hair twitched like fish in a
        net today

But it's not him or us I'm talking about – the Beloved's the only One
        here –
Each encouner with a lover on earth pays back some of our soul's deep
        debt today

My heart feels like a tunnel heavy with traffic from both worlds passing in
        space –
O *Ameen* – how did you get here – what conveyance? – I think it was by
        love not by jet today

5/12

31 ROAR OF THE LION

A lion roared but only a flea could hear it –
Only a flea that hid in the lion's mane could revere it

The roar of the lion is the ecstasy of its being
Announcing the appearance of the lion to anyone near it

Shadows on a hillside cast by the afternoon sun
Hide the lion in its natural camouflage – *so fear it!*

I put my head in the lion's mouth every day –
Love – O love! – I call out – if only you'd hear it!

Is the earth round and does it spin somewhat slowly in space?
The roar of God's lion completely surrounds the sphere of it –

It's the sun and moon on the earthly plane that light it –
But etherial light by Allah is what's needed to steer it

The flea became a roaring lion as well at last –
What was small became vast – *Ameen* – in the roar of pure spirit

5/12

32 PIRATE ON THE HIGH SEAS

A pirate on the high seas steals jewels –
His job in the workaday world is to conceal jewels

No need to enumerate the various precious kinds
But a pirate won't stand for anything but real jewels

He risks life and limb every moment – his fate at the gallows –
Going up over sides of heavily armed ships to find ideal jewels

The fact that he comes by them croodedly is irrelevant here –
He won't try to hijack a ship unless he feels *"jewels!"*

Each moment our hearts beat one way or another for love –
Toward physical survival or a spiritual rhythm that might yield jewels

God is Alive each moment – and He created us especially –
Mirrors of Himself to distribute since He only deals jewels

O Allah – the ship has heaved into view – and it's treasure-laden –
Knife in teeth – tears in eyes – let *Ameen* plunder passionate zeal's jewels

5/13

33 THE RESTAURANT WITH NO FOOD

We ate at a restaurant that had no food – we came to a world that has no
     world –
We put on our clothes and take off our bodies in this illusory appearance
     all-for-show world

I've saluted scarecrows – spoken to gravestones – flown with swallows to
     their springtime nests –
I've listened to wolves howl and heard howling wolf replies across vast
     empty space in a mountainous snow world

Did you come for fine dinners – silk garments from department stores – all
     the best silver and goblets of crystal?
It all passes through us without leaving a trace – or even an echo like light
     through a soft glow-world

The restaurant was empty of food – not a morsel – but the chairs were full
     as we waited for lunch –
The waiters went down the road – it took a half hour – we in a satisfied
     go-with-the-flow world

Once we've tasted our mother's milk – cuddled in her warm lap gurgled and
     cooed – the bond is incessant –
It takes a few weanings again and again – then slowly we realize there's
     another-to-know world

Get up from the empty restaurant – push back your chair –
Head straight for the door to the high not the low world

Ameen says "The staff has gone home and the sous chef's quit –
But Allah the Provider exists – as always – in His abundant zero world"

5/13

3 4 DESIRE

A gorgeous blond bombshell appeared who said her name was Desire
But I knew that wasn't her name though she said her name was Desire

The roadways are littered with corpses with vague smiles on their faces
Who were sacrificed what they thought was happily to the flame of Desire

Some are caught in the machinery and chopped into tiny bits
By the twists and turns and coils and dead-ends of the game of Desire

Even now the heart's not quite sure what to say about all this
Since there are various ways of shaping and acting on the same Desire

A turn to the right or a turn to the left may lead to a different end
Though if it turns out to be a disaster we always blame Desire

Let Allah be the single object – *Ameen* – as you plow your way –
And through every enticement let He alone be the One to claim your Desire

5/13

35 I'M NOT SAINT FRANCIS OF THE MOSQUITOS

for Asiyya Levin

There's a mosquito who's been buzzing near my ear this morning
Back and forth – I woke up when he landed feet first on my ear this
      morning

Tired from last night's *sohbet* that lasted until 2:30AM
I didn't set my alarm but would pray *Fajr* whenever it should appear this
      morning

I resisted the noise of his dentist's drill and slapped his landings
And finally woke up ten minutes after sunrise – I fear – this morning

Was he in fact an angel sent from the Throne of God to wake me?
Should I have taken him as beloved friend and addressed him as *"my dear"*
      this morning?

God gave them all a high-pitched buzzing sound they fly around using –
Whether it's a shrill satanic growl or the cry of a lover's longing isn't clear
      this morning

I know each one has a mother – and another mosquito might find it cute
But they're all blood-sucking vampires – which is spookily austere – this
      morning

Yet each thing in God's universe has a useful purpose for sure –
In the intricate workings of the world the one who woke me might be a
    divine gear this morning

I'll never know – one just landed on my arm and I got it in one swat –
Ameen – you're not Saint Francis of the mosquitos – though it may ruin
    your spiritual career this morning

5/14

36 I DIDN'T SLEEP BUT HAD WEIRD DREAMS

I didn't sleep but I had weird dreams on the way to Antalya –
I can't recall a single one of them – lost somewhere in the void on the
      way to Antalya

There are many puffy white and gray clouds in a bright blue sky
As we go by bus to spend the day in Antalya

Not sure why exactly – not going anywhere special –
Buy a few things – hoping as usual to attract a divine ray in Antalya

Bookstores – crowded streets – bus brakes – putt-putting motorbikes
The usual bustle of amazingly active ancient world cities –
      come-what-may in Antalya

Cloudburst – thunder – fat rainfall – drops briefly plummeting—
Lunch with God's lovers – then later – Turkish tea on a tray in Antalya

The day's not finished – *Ameen* – as you sit in a centuries old mosque
Listening for Allah – hearing birds outside – there's finally nothing
      left but *"Allah"* to say in Antalya

5/14

37 TWO LOVERS

Two lovers wanted to meet – so they sent each other love letters secretly –
As usual in these matters they feared the censure of others – so they sent
     their love letters secretly

Now a house on fire in a city never tries to hide its flames –
It burns openly and shamelessly – though it be set by fire-setters secretly

I don't say we should display our love for all to see
For there are subtleties of love that are often expressed better secretly

They wrote night and day until they both nearly passed out of their bodies
     completely
Drenching each word in rivers of tears that only got wetter and wetter –
     secretly

For in love they were like babies cradled in the motherly arms of the world
Held warm and tight – though they'd cut off all worldly fetters secretly

Love always has story within story and layer within layer
But if we peel away the details we'll find they're just minor aiders and
     abetters secretly

They'd known each other almost from birth though from different mothers
     separately –
Don't the twin valves of the heart reside together in a single breast secretly?

They met – they looked – they saw – they melted – it was all they knew
     – one was the sun the other the moon –
They traced each curved and straight line – each loop and dot – from A
     to Z – of the alphabet's letters secretly

In the mirrors of each other's hearts they saw no one else –
Each took care of the other's most intimate matters secretly

What peculiarities they imagined for themselves and what forbearance
     for the faults of the other!
Each other in each other's eyes more perfect – though ripped to passionate
     tatters secretly

The key is seeing the light in another even more strongly than in yourself –
Then you won't be swayed by any spiritual trend-setters secretly

The cups have been broken – the jug's been overturned – wine's flowing
     everywhere now –
But it can only be drunk by the free of heart – not by concept-netters
     secretly

Reading the words on the page they suddenly realized they were not each
     other at all –
They were non-existent by all normal guages and categorical inspectors
     secretly

One went off but came back again – unable to remain apart –
The ecstasy each felt in the other's presence gave them the spiritual stutters
     secretly

In the world of images lover and Beloved remain fixed in their places
      eternally –
But in the world of love it's the images that fluctuate like instant forgetters
      secretly

Each of our moments is like this – moving from one liquid world to another –
But not for a single moment are we actually Truth's quitters secretly

The teaching says only God exists – His love fills our hearts like a pump –
When the lovers searched for each other's forms they found nothing but
      love's glitters – secretly

Their letters were sent – they were joined in a breath – they were joined in
      death – they lived forever –
It's the end of a story that hasn't even begun – One Light – One heart –
      One God – in big letters – secretly

Ameen – you're tired – the night's been long – it's 2AM again – the story's
      endless –
Sleep now – though you try so hard to help openly through words those
      distracted love-debtors – secretly

5/15

38 FACE OF A LOVER

for Sitti Bajirah

In the dream I woke from the man told me I didn't have the face of a lover –
When I was sent away I didn't ask *"Why?"* – which is the disgrace of a lover

He said "Before I used to listen to you and I often learned so much –
But now you're in a state of dispairing gloom and not in the space of a
    lover"

I woke up sad but determined to reopen my petrified heart to love
So I sat and did vigorous *dhikr'Allah* as if in the race of a lover

Why do dreams come to us? Why do they follow like dark shadows over
    our hearts?
Maybe to grab their treetrunk and vigorously shake in the strong embrace of
    a lover

O Allah – please don't go off and leave me alone today – don't leave me
    behind!
Today we should think of nothing but love and Allah – and every trace
    of a lover

Everything else fades away insubstantially like vaporish wisps of blue smoke –
Only love and Allah remain after the full-blooded *"Erase!"* of a lover

So *Ameen* kick over your bad dream – note it – leave it – then go on –
Chase it away furiously once and for all with the spray-can Mace of a lover!

5/15

39 THERE'S NOWHERE ALLAH IS NOT

There's nowhere Allah is not – so this must be Paradise --
This boat on the choppy Mediterranean – a gust of Paradise

Leaving it all behind is not as easy as it sounds –
To be at ease in every moment – and *be just* in Paradise

A good word will do it – *"Allah is Powerful over everything!"*
Light comes into view – sound – colors – even beautiful *rust* in Paradise

We move along at a fast clip past the southern-most Turkish Alps –
Dark green trees – great blue shadows – creation's abundant lust in Paradise

Then sweet powdered apple cakes are passed around –
Nuts on top – crumbly and fruit-filled – with an almondy crust in Paradise

Ameen – you're still not a strong enough lover – your heart is veiled –
But if there were ever a perfect chance – now! – *trust* in Paradise!

5/15

40 TURTLE

The small turtle I met on the top of the primeval hill was chewing a long
      grassblade –
I greeted him – he gave me a slow reptilian glance – kind of sidelong his
      grassblade –

We chatted a while – exchanged perceptions – then he decided to go –
Even as a turtle it didn't take much time at all to trudge off among
      grassblades

The fir trees on that summet between two blue Mediterranean coves stood
      apart at shadowy angles –
I expected white centaurs and laughing satyrs to appear with diaphanous
      wood nymphs singing songs of grassblades

Love talked among the trees – love stalked off with the turtle – love sank
      into its balmy afternoon splendor –
Love passed like a breath among thistles and thorn brambles – among weak
      and strong grassblades –

Faruk's right – no moment exists without Allah – no moment bereft – no
      moment missing –
Ameen – our lives also nibble contentedly and thoughtfully on lifelong
      grassblades!

5/15

41   SINGLE STEP FORWARD

There's a long trip to be taken on a short road – if you're ready to
      turn on the light –
The doorway is already around us – knob in hand – *O Allah* –
      turn on the light!

This time it's not poison to drink the thick liquor of our lives –
Like the black stone of the *Kaaba* – it's really an urn full of light

Liquor of ourselves poured out into various bodies –
But the soul in us is one – burning with Allah's true light

Shall we send out for the usual doctor? He'll come on a slow donkey –
He's only a carpenter for broken bones – with a lot to learn from
      the light

Sink the ship of the *nafs* – *Ameen* – and walk out on the water –
When you pass leave just what's essential – let no one mourn
      for your light!

5/15

42 ROOSTER

A rooster crows and its head turns into a shrill birthplace full of roses –
The sun of love comes up and the whole world becomes a space full of
roses

Is it just one giant rose extending from the beginning of time to now?
The Prophet Muhammad was there before Adam – by God's Grace full of
roses

So many windows looking out on the garden tended by servants of light –
Each moment coming to flower with time's clock face full of roses

I can't get away from the song of the rose – *Habib – Mevlana – Bawa
– Dede – Yunus*
And Faruk who attracts with a magnetic burning love's embrace full of
roses

We float like petals on the ocean of love from continent to continent –
When the rooster of dawn wakes us up countries vanish in a rising
staircase full of roses

Ameen – hey! – needless to say – right now everything's coming up roses –
No need to go anywhere – all moments here – no moment needs to
displace the chaste pull of roses!

5/15

43 LAST MORNING IN TURKEY

Last morning in Turkey – birds chortling in trees – cocks crowing –
      as they will tomorrow –
We'll be on a plane back to Philadelphia following God's will
      tomorrow

There's all this jumpy electric activity in a cell just before division –
It's been like this for us – one delirious cell – all in one place – till
      tomorrow

We'll be gone – but the sky will be blue or gray – fleecy or clear –
Water will gush from mountaintops into various rivers and rills –
      tomorrow

But when you're with Allah in a burning heart place doesn't matter –
The fear of course is whether our hearts will be so heavenly filled
      tomorrow

Allah is in all place and no place at once – not limited by time –
We as His lovers must climb heart's rugged and smooth hill tomorrow

Oh I don't know what I'm talking about – all I know is love caught
      fire among us!
Our guide has stars for eyes – Paradise for a smile – with enough light
      to fill tomorrow

I won't talk about his secret or inner path – only Allah knows that
      for sure –
I wouldn't even have words nor my pen enough ink in its quill
      tomorrow!

Let this burning continue – Allah – it's Yours – don't let it die down in
    our hearts –
You've given us health beyond our expectations – don't let us get ill
    tomorrow

Ameen – it's over – it's done – he said *"Don't wait till the end"* –
    it won't end –
Go like a pillar of light on legs – like a heart that's tranquil and still –
    tomorrow

5/16

44 THE PIVOT

When you're wandering around with a pivot there's blessings in merely
     circulating –
You may go nowhere – do nothing – nothing pressing – merely circulating

How many planets can the universe hold? How many lights can the
     heart?
It's Allah First and Last – Hidden and Manifest – world's dressing
     merely circulating

A man of God buys shoes in the market – tries hats – sips tea
     – answers his cell phone –
Is it he or is it He Who is doing the talking – the looking – the leather
     caressing – *merely circulating?*

If the center of the universe were to open up would it be any different?
     Allah is always Allah –
But such a *no one* as this who walks and talks like a normal man – watch
     out! – Light's eye is assessing by merely circulating

The pivot is a center everything circles around – it's a matter of pure
     rotation!
A pivot man simply circles round Allah – the Central Point of all
     – obsessed with merely circulating

"Don't look at the man in front of you – look at Me!" he said – *Ameen*
     (Ameen! Ameen!)
In this life always hold to Allah and a saint of Allah – whose lesson is
     merely circulating

5/16

45 SCISSORS

They inspected my bags in the Istanbul airport and confiscated my
      scissors –
I'd forgotten when I was packing my suitcase I should have relocated my
      scissors

Light is single and undifferentiated in spiraling sheets through creation –
Then cut into shapes of each particular thing as if articulated by scissors

But how intricate our life with its mechanical details of *now this now that!*
Rather than sitting in blesséd stillness as if complicated by scissors

The skies are decorated with clouds and vapors floating like veils –
Then suddenly a bank of cutout white clouds as if created by scissors

Now I know Ben Jonson said of Shakespeare *"Would he had blotted
      a thousand"* of his words –
But then the super-Godly abundance in his work might drain out as if
      underrated by scissors

But of course I'm naturally in favor of maximum rather than minimum
      expression –
Too severe a cutting for me would make our songs of praise obfuscated by
      scissors

Ameen when you get home go to the nearest drugstore and buy yourself
      a new pair of scissors -
Simple ones – nothing fancy or expensive – not even necessarily nickel-
      plated scissors

5/17

46 NEARLY LANDING

The plane's an hour away from landing in New York – soon we'll be
  home –
The island of light we've been on for two weeks – our soul's refugee
  home

Isn't it always in the heart anyway – from earliest beginning to end?
That wherever we are with the heart's eye open we always see home?

In the electric embrace of the arms of Mevlana in his tomb I'd arrived –
"Welcome" he said – *"I've been waiting for years"* – in eternity's home

I sank into blindness – deafness and death for an instant – all praise to
  Him!
For this perhaps – from our body – our self – we have to flee home

In the jostle and bustle of the plane – people getting ready to land –
From God's land of life and light to God's land of light and life
  – heaven's earthly home

Ameen – to see yourself you must flee yourself – miles in an instant – at
  once!
Always turn round the central pivot – and you'll always *be* home!

5/17

PART 2

AMERICA

47 BRILLIANT CORNERS

Brilliant corners – blooming trees – skies of shouts of joy – *pure light!*
There's no escape from here except through successive doorways of *Your*
    Light!

A touch so gentle even gnats feel safe under the tenderness of its weight –
A face so open nothing more is hidden except the secret lure of Light

If the heavens are plazas where saints walk – show me the steps!
This worlds needs nothing so much as it needs just a cure of light –

Having drunk the water – the milk – and the wine of Paradise on earth
O God – now please serve these slaves of Yours only a sure Light!

It's the chance we must take to keep love's heart open wide to all –
Standing in the shadow that true resplendence makes of our poor light

The tongue is everything – the tip of the tongue that tastes wordlessness –
So stunned – it's only by tasting that the soul can endure light –

Only those who obstruct the lovers' Path to Allah – by whatever means –
Those are the greatest evildoers – those who injure light –

We've been with ones who lead to the highest door and open it wide –
They're the latest messengers from the Source – they ensure light

Ameen – it's begun now – in a new place that's no place – though it be home –
The heart's arch reaches down into heaven – and up into Nūr – *Light!*

5/18
(*Philadelphia*)

48 A LEOPARD-SHAPED FLAME

A flame in the shape of a leopard leapt into space and ignited –
A heart sweetened with God's Name repeatedly quickend its pace and
      ignited –

A beloved friend came along nonchalantly looking as normal as anyone –
But an "anyone" not as a mask but a mirror – we looked into his face and
      ignited!

The earth is a ball of spirit – not matter – it rolls on long breaths and sighs –
It swims among stars and galaxies God spun fine as lace – then ignited

A question was asked of us – before any of us was born – before the world
      was formed –
"Who is your Lord?" – And we replied *"You!"* – now resonant space is ignited

Was it really so long ago? Before any matter at all was created?
Its echoes linger just a little behind us – meanings giving us chase –
      re-ignited

We stand in our heights whatever they may be – interiors and exteriors as
      they are –
No ones in no place – never were – never will be – only Allah – in a place
      that's ignited!

Ameen – these moments are dense and transparent – light and dark at once –
The task through it all is to be in an awed and bewildered interspace
      – ignited!

5/19

49 THE PHONE RINGS

The phone rings – it's a dear friend recently divorced – quailing in tears –
She has to find a school for her son – her ex blocking her – she's flailing in
    tears

Last night on TV a special on Muhammad Ali showed his courage in ring
    and life –
Holding to Allah against unjust authority – prevailing in tears

Where's God's giant bird swooping from the sky to take off all our troubles?
The heart in adversity shows world championship strength – never failing in
    tears

My wife upstairs talks to her – follows her rollercoaster up hill and down –
She's a master of good counsel – administering balm – Florence
    Nightengaling her tears

Our life is a chessboard where a master of *dhikr* is pitted against foes –
Checkmate may be by cool strategy – only now and then assailing in tears

Allah's mercy comes in the spaces between – and in the spaces themselves!
Inhaling God's Name in difficulty – then exhaling in tears

Ameen – sitting up in bed – rainy day outside – jetlag slowly disappearing –
The boats of the heart heading out in glorious weather – or sailing –
    in tears...

5/19

50 FLUTE NOTE

If a flute note could bring you near again – as the presence fades
I would blow its wailing poignancy across all distance – as the presence
       fades

Bridges of white egrets in stationary flight arc from land mass to land mass
Carrying the song more strongly from heart to heart – as the momentary
       present-tense fades

For you are here with me as much as you'll ever be and as long as forever –
Radiating the splendor of Hidden secrets – as materiality's pretense fades

Towers of topazes – windows of rose quartz – turquoise domes – the call
       to prayer –
There is just no way that something of such heart-rending magnificence
       fades

My mouth is still filled with the sweetness of your kisses – strong aftertaste
       of roses –
My heartbeats resound with a deeper rhythm – even as direct evidence
       fades

But that's not quite true – *"Everywhere you turn you see the Face of Allah"*—
Ah, let that truth become emblematically stronger – as all contrary
       coalescence fades

Ameen – in the corridor of the ruined arena – listening to the crowd –
Those shades who have passed before us – what is subtle remains –
       what is dense – fades!

5/19

5 1   I WAKE UP

I wake up in the middle of the night still inside the same body –
After travels to color-drenched lands – I return inside the same body –

Flying over trees by moonlight – past wheatfields with flying sheep –
Darting freely over mirror-clear pools – a dragonfly with a flame body!

Standing in the doorway of the lavish court of Emperor Ming on some
       ministerial errand –
Able to change shape into spinning wheel – towering tower – just a real
       trickery game body!

Even going so far perhaps – since the soul in sleep seems so completely
       free and arbitrary –
That in the dream-world of zero gravity – I might even appear in some
       beautiful dame's body

A peacock fanning its celestial tail – an elephant the size of night trumpeting
       its grief –
A wild lion standing on a hilltop roaring – then reducing its animal rage
       into a tame body

Soul completely innocent and amorphous – doing good everywhere in
       love's clutches –
Floating like a cloud in love's embraces – without being locked in a
       praise or blame body!

Hurtling over mountaintops – and especially the mountaintops of our
  baser selves –
Showing our pure heart what soul can be like once it overcame body!

So I was water and jug – lake and hollow – air and breather of air –
  song but no singer –
Then after timelessness turned back into time – *Ameen* once more –
  became body

5/20

52 IN THE DARK

In the dark everything is nothing – when the light's on – *boom!* – every little
    thing seems real –
There's the bed – the floor – books in piles – colors – shapes – every little
    thing seems real!

Night is Layla – the Beloved – in undifferentiated beauty behind her veil
    of purest unity –
Her eyes flash like planetary spheres – her single clear voice makes all our
    many dreams real

When you see the ocean you think – *"This is the one original element on
    earth!"* –
Great liquid mother of creation – but Who makes all her various watery
    streams real?

In our hearts the thought of nothingness is like standing on a sheer cliff in a
    high wind –
But the next thought – of God's Unity throughout creation – makes all the
    next world's otherworldly gleams real!

There are things – then there are none – there is us – then we are gone –
Is it eternity's endless blackness or is it multiple rainbow glories? Are all the
    spectrum's wild extremes real?

This world with all its complications – glorious grand operas and ridiculous
    opera buffos –
We gear up to live forever – taking life just as it is – but death makes none
    of its mortal schemes real

Our hearts are the unifiers – love is the "unified theory" of everything –
  Allah is always Alone –
Ameen – thoughts vanish – but hearts beat on – God's single light is what
  makes our trillion flashing eye-beams real!

5/21

53　FACE

He has a face that explodes into light like a sweet supernova –
It illuminates everyone and everything around him – like a sweet
　　　supernova

His eyes become stronger and deeper even as they seem to disappear –
His smile scatters diamonds in space like an upbeat supernova

How can what is non-physical in nature come through a physical
　　　presence?
A singular totality in a human body that is yet somehow like a
　　　complete supernova?

How did God decide to bless one of His slaves – one of us –
　　　in this loving way?
It's a love affair for sure between what lives and dies – and He
　　　Who does not die – endlessness and a fleet supernova

Those who are near want to stay near like every baby at the teet
　　　of its mother –
For pure honey comes out of those starry lips in deeply-dipped words –
　　　like a replete supernova

We lock star-debris and float for a while amost free of gravity
　　　through the night
Tumbling together in open love – though veiled by darkness –
　　　a discreet supernova

These people float through our world – but they're not really there –
  there is only Allah –
They are complete – Allah is complete – while our world's like an
  incomplete supernova

Ameen – in America the same effect can be had – even from so far away
  from his place –
It's known as the radiant smile and light-exploding face of your own
  heartbeat supernova

5/22
(*first line received in a dream*)

54 LISTEN TO THE ELEPHANT BELLS

Listen to the elephant bells – the flute – and the tree branches –
This love won't let me sleep – I'm scraping back and forth like
    wind-swept tree branches

Rain comes – roots drink greedily – tree storing water in its trunk –
An elephant wraps *its* trunk around it looking for free branches

Allah's so generous He won't let me sleep but He gives me this poem –
Allah the Source of true silence and sound – we're His forgery branches

The restless heart goes into the dark looking for brilliance –
Little by little leaving the periphernalia of this world's illusory branches

Commotion from a distant dimension pulls us like a celestial magnet
And draws us to the central core through one of its vapory branches

Allah ignites us – Allah excites us – to come to Him alone
With the courtesy of a passionate lover who observes His boundary's
    branches

"Closer than the jugular vein" – ah – not far off beyond some ocean horizon –
Not distant – not disinterested – but whispering here in my arterys'
    branches

The world is heartbeating inside my chest tonight – for as long as I live –
Ameen – go to sleep – a little sleep at least is one of life's compulsory
    branches!

5/22

55 A PRECIOUS FRIEND'S TREASURE

for Musa Muhaiyuddeen

I lost a precious friend's treasure he'd entrusted to me trustingly –
Poems he'd written in a true inspired state then entrusted to me trustingly

I was meant to take the legal pad home and type them out for him –
I put the pad on the top of the car and forgot when I drove away –
      thoughtlessly – trustingly

Lucky they were short and Oh so sweet – so he could remember them one
      by one
But somewhere in our heaven a star blinked out – hopefully just for a
      moment – to shine again happily – trustingly

The universe and my vigilance had always been well-sealed against disaster –
I could jump as high as possible in the air and know I'd land safe – like a
      flea – trustingly

I set it on top of the car and thought *"What a place to forget it!"* then
      promptly forgot it!
It was me – not some demon – since Allah made me recipient and trustee –
      trustingly

We move forward in the dark with feelers twitching not knowing what will
      come
But when something – an object – a bond of loving friendship – gets lost –
      even for a moment – it's piracy – *trust me!*

If it hadn't been *poems* – socks – money – pills – even his cell phone! –
But they were handwritten gnomic gems of inspiration I'd been encouraging
     carefreely – trustingly!

I don't know what jewel from Samarkand or sweet intoxicating nectar from
     Paradise I could bring to heal our bond
But *Ameen* – from deepest heart – resort now to sincere bribery – trustingly

5/23

56 AT THE EDGE OF SLEEP

At the edge of sleep where no grass even grows I hear a faint call –
Is it from sheep-filled meadow or the Next World? Oh such a quaint call!

Knobs on the doors are cold to the touch – windows fill with fire –
In the volcanic fury of daily existence – listen to the saint call!

A warbling as of birds – a faucet-running sound of water –
A creaking door suddenly becomes clear as it lodges its complaint call

Allah pure beyond any description – though we've been given Your Word –
Open us like a single door from heart to heart to answer Your *without
        restraint* call

Maybe the one that keeps us in life – the subtle *Allah Latif* call –
At least it's proven to be the *one that's hard to sing or paint* call!

If I dive down into sleep again will I be able to answer it?
Ameen – whether it's strong or not is irrelevant – it's a pre-birth *ordained* call

                                                5/24

57 WINGS

Travel to a place like Turkey for Allah's sake gives your heart wings –
Travel to anywhere for Allah's sake gives your heart wings

But especially if at your destination is a heart-guide whose face is a light –
With a few words (and glasses of tea) he gives you state-of-the-art wings

There once was a light in a forest day and night no one could explain –
Was it butterflies coming from all over vibrating their fluttery-smart wings?

When we see someone face to face whose face is a radiant effulgence
Do we actually open our own selves with our deepest intention's counterpart
    wings?

There once was a mirror in a forest day and night standing still and alone –
The utter receptivity of its divine reflection alone was able to impart wings

I just took a journey around the room and came back and sat down –
Allah – Who is nowhere and everywhere at once – *be mine!* Give Your
    sweetheart wings!

Now get up and do the dawn prayer to Allah – Your Beloved here and
    everywhere –
When it's time to say the final *Ameen* – may you depart *wings!*

5/25

58   OUTSIDE OF YOU

Ameen – where did you get the idea that everything's outside of you?
If that's true then consciousness has no meaning and everything's
    outside of you –

Comings and goings – meetings and partings – mountains and seas –
The bell-like sound of each of God's creatures rings outside of you?

Doorways are not to go through then but only rectangles onto the void!
The choir of the past as well as the future sings outside of you?

You wash your hands and arms and feet to get ready for prayer –
But do you think for a moment the dirt of this world only clings to
    outside of you?

Moonrise golden and yellow – with its vast searchlight of white –
Sunset with its lengthening shadows and the soft tranquility it brings –
    outside of you?

The body's dimensions are nothing – in fact – in actual reality –
Motions in waves or particles flow easily as if from seemingly outside
    of you?

Neither one nor the other – neither this nor that – neither true – *only
    Allah!*
Heart-bursting frontiers made solid by mind shattering what's outside
    of you!

Ameen – it's over – the clock's reached midnight – all hands pointing
    upward –
All's One – Alif – Unity – Oh really! – in reality *nothing's* outside of you!

5/25

59 SWEET GUIDE

O sweet Guide transform me further – make me a duck with her ducklings –
An eagle with her eaglets in their nest – *O I don't care!*

A seawall for the ocean to crash against day and night –
A lake to reflect the sky and all the rest – *O I don't care!*

Sixty-one years from my birth and I've leapt through a few fiery hoops of
   transformation –
But now erase all familiar traces and leave only Allah – the best –
   O I don't care!

A rock on the road to keep folks from falling over the side –
A meadow up and down hills for wild horses to run on with zest –
   O I don't care!

A lone face in a mirror whose light's cast from a burning heart –
So what if the whole thing goes up in fiery sparks – we're God's guests –
   so I don't care!

Simple things – a water drop – a steam drop – even nothing at all –
Just say the word dear Transformer – nothing suppressed – *O I don't care!*

Even my asking's a sin – it means I'm still here – someone making the
   request!
Ah *Ameen* – here or nowhere – alive or dead – in every case we're blessed –
   so I don't care!

5/25

60 THROW OPEN THE TAVERN DOORS

Throw open the tavern doors – let the tepid drinkers out and the heavy
     drinkers in – it's time for love!
Walls of icy crystal – roof of stars – doors and floors of our breaths – *it's time
     for love!*

The road is long and winds through dangerous groves – devils abound –
A few stops between treacherous blackouts – *ah begone!* – it's overtime for
     love!

Give us strong drink to boil the heart and shake all frenzy loose –
Throw all heady spices in – sage rosemary and thyme – for love!

On second thought forget the drinks! – the atmosphere – the talk!
I want the ancient tavern-keeper Himself – Who knows by heart the secret
     recipe to the sublime – for love!

To sit among the hardened drunks at the front table etched and carved with
     Names –
In the most disreputable corner of the place – *as if it were a crime to love!*

I've seen their eyes – hot burning coals – their faces – extra-planetary suns!
Each one's been scorched by all the chords and colors and heart's hard
     rhymes – for love!

The forest it's in – the mountains beyond – it's all a giant tavern with its
     own moon – its own day –
The whole reeling universe of drunken song provides the highest paradigm –
     for love!

This is no petty company – these passionate drinkers have lost everything
    they own –
They've thrown their selves – their fates – their entire world – into pure
    quicklime – *for love!*

O *Ameen* – out of the depths of darkness dank odors and smoke – this
    deathly world –
Take hands with these whispering desperados – and start to climb – *for love!*

5/26

61 THE HOLY GRAIL

They looked for the Holy Grail in all the wrong places – they left home
   when they should have stayed home –
They wandered away from protected precincts into territories of mortal
   combat and terror – when they should have stayed home!

Turn a corner in your house – slit your eyes in the light – see! – *there it
   sits!*
On a window sill – with eternal radiance shining through its tissue-thin
   sides – like a perfect jade home –

You enter inside a common corridor – one you've been down before a
   thousand times –
But this time you see things differently – not just defined by the usual
   light-and-shade home

Heart's business – doorways inside doorways – floodgates within floodgates –
God's chalice of light sits high in the rush of its waterfall cascade home

The battle for Jerusalem where so many have died is the inbreath of our
   natural breathing –
The outbreath of remembrance of *Haqq* glides through every checkpoint
   barricade home

The sweet spoils are always life and light – holding God's goblet high and
   praising The Living One –
Abd al-Hayy – Slave of The Living One – it's time to bring the true crusade
   home!

5/26

62 DOOR

Dear Lord – five times a day we stop everything to face Your door –
Five times a day we try to draw close by turning to face Your door

We put the world behind us as our hands go down from our ears –
We stand straight on our own two feet in the place of Your door

Are You there behind it as it faces us – do You hear our pleas?
His Message assures us Your Presence really does grace Your door!

But what is it – this direction we face away from our selves and the
       world?
That only one thing remain as our selves begin to efface – *Your door!*

You're nowhere else – being everywhere and nowhere – as we disappear –
We stand the exact shape of ourselves in the divine space of Your door!

We stand and bow and prostrate until our hearts are above our heads –
Our hearts incessantly beating for reply – Truth's embrace – at Your
      door!

If the whole earth is a mosque for us – hills – valleys – plains – the
      living-room floor –
Yet to stop and turn where there is nothing visible – *ah!* – nothing can
      replace Your door!

It's not of this world – it's Yours alone – Allah – the dimension of prayer
      heart to heart –
World falls away – we're suspended in space – it's a celestial staircase –
      Your door!

And in the prayer we say *ameen* – and *"Peace be upon you!"* at the end –
And after the prayer we leave nothing behind – no physical trace – but
    Your door!

And as we approach – step by step – heartbeat by heartbeat – to adore –
We hope to catch at least a fleeting glimpse of Your resplendent Face –
    Your door!

                                      5/27

63 MOURNING DOVE

The Mourning Dove makes a soft cooing sound like a maid lamenting
      her laundry – *hu hu hu hu hu!*
The rosebud makes a sound like the rustling of costly silk fresh from
      God's laundry – *hu hu hu hu hu!*

High in the Atlas peaks by a pool that reflects nothing but the sky's silver –
In a cluster of leaves blooms a blue Forget-me-not – whispering her name
      to all and sundry – *hu hu hu hu hu!*

Stars blow kisses to each other across gloomy dark – stardust floating
      between –
There's a congeneity of love that holds all things in its embrace – nothing
      squandered – *hu hu hu hu hu!*

Do you think it's just dust beneath your feet – inanimate and dead?
But it was once people – civilizations – mountains that wandered –
      hu hu hu hu hu!

I heard a mockingbird on a pole near Atlantic City imitate seagulls cawing –
Ah – God's consciousness afloat in everything – even *that* winged vagabond –
      hu hu hu hu hu!

The universe wakes and sleeps – wakes and sleeps – its great boundaryless
      eye opens –
God never sleeps – in the tiniest atom His Light is in – and way beyond –
      hu hu hu hu hu!

Ameen – as usual – love's let you hear birds this morning chirping in their
trees –
Bewilderment at God's magnificence has put you in this quandary –
hu hu hu hu hu!

5/29

64 LAGOON

A voice drifts from the space of an incredibly near lagoon
Calling all lovers together from wherever they are to this indelibly dear
    lagoon

Qais al-Qarni is our man – whose love for the Prophet was so intense –
Like us he never saw him with physical eyes – but his love was a vast and
    clear lagoon

We drift over land and sea – our hearts giant wind-sails or outpouring
    waterfalls –
Sparkling waters from many rivers entering a single sincere lagoon

It wakes us in the night – it hits us in the day as we're walking along –
This call – like the sirens – or a Lorelei – from some invisible frontier
    lagoon

God made our hearts like this – a space like an ear to hear Him wherever
    we are –
We turn toward it as if listening to a music-of-the-spheres lagoon!

It's joy – it's light – a festival of compassion that starts directly from this
    point –
Like sunshine sparkling through the leaves of a forest – it's not an austere
    lagoon

Ameen – heed it – it's not far off – it's immediate – ah listen – *it's right now!*
Each of God's creatures hears it – love's sweet melting-heart oxygen
    atmosphere lagoon!

5/30

65 OPALESCENT SOUL

As humans we have so many things to look after – our nails – our hair –
    our hearts – our transcendent souls –
We file our nails – we cut our hair – we fall in love or find the true object
    of the love of our resplendent souls –

A camel stands in silhouette in moonlight on a desert horizon – majestic
    and nobly still –
The whole scene taken in by our eyes of love – ancient dimension of our
    luminescent souls!

I see you over the wall in your garden so tenderly tending your red and
    yellow roses –
You move so slowly you might be a ghost – the most vivid thing your
    bright quiescent soul

If we veer too far to the left we might founder – if we veer too far to the
    right we might turn to stone –
The frenzy of movement from side to side is the wild animal of our
    adolescent souls –

I just ate an animal cracker from the bag – it's hard to tell what it is – it
    might be a horse –
The fuzzy and insecure outlines of so many folk show the sad sinking of
    deeply depressant souls

The door opens and light pours in – in a flash we're past gross physical
    being and gone –
Our own outlines disappear altogether engulfed by our death-angel's
    incandescent soul

O heart – lift up your sleepy eyelids and look out through the darkling
    trees!
Wildflowers burst into firework blooms of your efflorescent soul!

Dive down *Ameen* – through air earth and water – pass through infernos
    of fire!
In the depths where sunlight rarely falls – you'll find your original
    opalescent soul!

5/30

66 TINY SOAP BUBBLE

As I was washing dishes tonight a tiny soap bubble from the sponge
        drifted past my eyes
Like a slow snowflake drifting down this shiny round universe rose and
        drifted past my eyes

I said *hello* to it – so alive it seemed – and on a definite quest –
Colors and lights from the room reflected on its surface and shifted past
        my eyes –

A universe inside it – a universe outside – thin membrane of soap in
        between –
Where – with all its invisible inhabitants – was it going – uplifted past
        my eyes?

Allah held it both inside and out – light on both sides resplendently shining –
My heart was amazed by this little almost immaterial thing – aloft and
        adrift past my eyes

It floated on an updraft I suppose – in its gentle arc in the air –
I might not have noticed such a tiny thing at all – if it hadn't been gifted to
        my eyes

It went directly to its destiny – the countertop – and landed –
A moment later it was gone – the world had barely sniffed it – past my eyes –

Stop everything – *Ameen* – stand still – you're afloat on a similar arc!
God's light on both sides of you – mortality and immortality – divinely
        gearshifted past your eyes!

5/31

67 A WORM AS LONG AS LIFE IS

There's a worm as long as life is wriggling along on earth –
It's a fat and healthy happy worm – wriggling along on earth

There's a moon with a variable face glowing in the sky –
Sometimes it looks like it's pursing its lips and singing a song on earth

There's a butterfly with the face of a human being fluttering out of a wood –
Its lightness and delicate flight is the opposite of hitting a gong on earth

Shadows of migrating herds of bison loom over the ground –
They stretch from one end to the other in a giant oblong on earth

I wish I knew how to free myself and others from this time-bound track –
Allah alone can remove us from the imprisoning material throng on earth

Light that can chop down redwoods and reconstitute them alive as before –
Can flit like a gnat on an updraft or crash like King Kong on earth

Somehow – *Ameen* – though not of this world – the lover's sigh and longing
Lifting from death and singing praises – is what should belong on earth

5/31

68 ONE MORE DRINK

One more drink – tavern's closing – chairs upturned on the tables of love –
Top up my glass – tonight I want to warrant all the wildest labels of love –

Windows blink closed – fountains stop – even the wind's dying down –
I'm with the moths circling the lights – catching the last towering Babels of
    love

Let night go – let day go too while you're at it – it's all eternity now –
wingéd horses – all colors of the rainbow – whinny now in the stables of
    love

Black sky turns blue – dark clouds fan to sun – air swirls in a coil –
Hot air balloon heartbeats arise – held aloft by the aching cables of love

It's dark and smoky in here – most drinkers are gone – the place has
    emptied out –
But even at this hour you can hear the echoes of the battling Cains and
    Abels of love

Yes – even that murder love's murder – even that evil was love's crime –
God-love turned yellow with jealousy – Cain's heart totally disabled by love

This is getting extreme now – wine fumes are rising – wild pictures float –
Romeos and Juliets – Laylas and Majnuns – all the majestic fables of love!

All right – I'll go home – my Lord's House has many mansions it's said –
Ameen – off with you now! – *go!* – to His House of Seven Gables of love

5/31

69 TREE

I've spent an eternity looking out the window at the fluttering leaves of our
    tree
It's a young red Japanese Maple – breeze quivering the graceful recitatives
    of our tree

Eternity might not be the right word – I'm back here writing it down –
But time seemed to stop – I was carried back to the Adams and Eves of the
    tree

It's in our blood – this timelessness – even as it beats in time –
Our hearts – though – live suspended in space – where eternity cleaves to
    the tree

Our mortal breaths and our mortal bodies beat footprints through the
    world
And tragic entanglements – mistakes and their hopelessness – all of this
    grieves the tree

A moment of pure wonder lasts forever – it flies free of beginnings and ends –
Then I'm not so sure it's only our single self alone who perceives the tree

The air is packed with invisible presences – djinn good and bad – and angels –
Saints who bend to help us may be the fluttering sleeves of the tree

A tree whose branches are all our lives – our job – to go down to the roots –
Our obstacles only our idiosyncrasies whose webbing weaves through the
    tree

It's there at the window – first tree of creation – and also the one in our yard –
Allah Creator of Eternity in time – to see who sees through the tree

Ameen – the eyes of your heart in space receiving guests while a guest
     yourself…
One glimpse all you need (enough for one who believes) of the tree

                                                                6/2

70 YESTERDAY OR TOMORROW?

Am I in yesterday or tomorrow? I just opened my eyes from somewhere
    to here –
There was a large fired clay sculpture – soft blues and tans – totally
    disappearing between somewhere to here –

It's just before sunset prayer – the spirits are fleeing – their long sleeves
    elegantly flowing
Night is rolling its huge carpet of black velvet across the air – to here

The sphinx sits in the gathering dark – her paws in front of her in the sand –
Her ruined face with its broken nose and eternally fixed stare – to here

Red lights bobbing way out at sea – green moonlight – white paths in the
    water –
It seems all the worlds are suddenly gathered – bending like a single flare –
    to here

I rub my eyes and an intricate stained glass window appears –
A little illuminated vision that came without any fanfare – to here

Chuang Tzu's butterfly – a real thing in a dream or a dream in reality?
I'd hate to have to fill out a verifiable questionnaire – to here

Guides – saints – prophets – walis – extend *Ameen* your steady hands
And let me fly in love's flame – Allah's own *boutonnière* – to here!

6/2

71 LOVERS MEET AT NIGHT

Lovers meet at night when everyone's asleep – they wear shoes of doeskin –
    their hands are flame –
Behind walls – in dark alleys – at the edges of forests – their demands are
    flame

Their lips have said all the words – their lips have trembled into silence –
Their bodies are torches that light up the night – even their innermost
    glands are flame

What is it that attracts them so when this burning's so utterly intense?
They avoid the water that would douse their love – preferring to remain
    firebrands of flame

They've become shrines for each other's worship – at the top is a heart
    vase of fire –
Up steps of blood rose-quartz and bone-crystal – veritable Holy Lands
    of flame

No distance too great for these lovers to cross to see each other face
    to face –
God's Face not more sweet to them since it's God's Face they seek –
    in their Neverlands of flame

No hardship too great – *Ameen* – in the normal grit of every day –
In the hourglass of love – what falls through the tiny eye of space is
    time's granulated sands of flame

6/3

7 2 BICYCLE

Night comes in like a fat black baby on a bright green bicycle
Crunching across million dollar bills laid on a highwire – on a bright
      phosphorene bicycle

I think I would like to see everything in the world the way whales see –
They seem to plow through the oceans as if on a serene bicycle

Lotuses grow up from murky depths of reflecting pools –
The light dazzles all around them as if bounced off a Celestine bicycle

Prophetic messages in lesser form waft into our hearts all the time –
They pedal in almost singing to themselves as if on an unforeseen bicycle

"Let's go for a ride!" Night says to the lover who's burning with love –
"We'll rush through heaven and earth in our quest for the Beloved on my Mean
      Machine *bicycle!"*

Heartbeats from before the creation – heartbeats of Noah above the
      Flood –
They beat and boom inside us like a *Begin the Beguine* bicycle

The lover doesn't want to sleep a wink in case the Beloved happens by –
The lover wants to sail through the earth all night on a caffeine bicycle!

Don't just pedal in space like a windmill – don't just lean against a wall –
Be a vehicle of rapid advancement to Allah – O night – be *Ameen's* bicycle!

6/3

73 ROAR OF A LION

Does the roar of a lion engulf the lion as much as it engulfs a gazelle?
Or does he broadcast his megaphone roar hoping to engulf a gazelle?

Does the doer sever all connection with his deed once it's out in the world?
Does leaping have nothing at all to do with it – or is it the better half of
gazelle?

The lion of night surrounds us all – we disappear in its roar –
Is there nothing at all left of us then – are we the epitaph of gazelle?

Is Allah His Names? His Presence? When he says *"Be!"* to us is *He not?*
His whispering Eye of True Vision can eternally photograph gazelle

We love to make actions that fly off us like birds let out of their cages
But we can't just hope to put the results on a figurine shelf of gazelle

Touch air – touch water – touch generosity – touch love –
These things named always lead to their Namer – from adoring seraph
to gazelle

Ameen – dive into dolphin-filled waters – browse with gnus in the sun –
This world a clear picture of God – Unseen One – with His abundant
wealth of gazelle

6/4

THE WAY WE MOVE ALONG

People move in their bodies as they must – striding or shuffling along –
You want to get out there and sing a song as they morosely shuffle along

Youths in overly baggy clothes – I don't see how they can walk at all –
But though they swagger now – later in life I see them garfluffling along

We all have a particular shape – stick figures set in motion a certain way –
Some roll as they walk – some sidle – others just flow ear-muffling along

We enter this life with a genetic anatomy from various relatives living or
    dead –
One walks like his pioneer grandpa – one like her slave great grandma
    in calico ruffling along

We carry the jewels of our ancestors in the way they moved through this
    very world –
Precious gestures somehow immortalized in our stance with a bit of
    reshufflng along

At the end of the day we resemble them too in their attitude of quiet repose –
Die before you die – *Ameen* – then the Voice of God won't just go muffling
    along

6/4

75 A MAN ON THE ROAD TO GOD

I met a man on the road to God with the intense face of an owl –
I felt the closeness of diamond-white feathers in the perfect space
    of an owl

Eyes of divine penetration burn all the way into our souls –
And ignite us in a blaze of love – the secret grace of an owl

Now the owl is not revered universally as being spiritually wise –
In some places *"owl"* means *"stupid"* – what abject disgrace for an owl!

Once I was walking in the woodsy hills above Bolinas Bay in California
And a white owl landed in a treetop in a clearing and stared hard at me –
    a real ace of an owl!

I may be thinking of that owl when I say this man was owl-like to me –
Maybe in primordial Paradise they're the same – original birthplace of
    an owl

My heart opened at this person's gaze on the road to a Beloved God –
Love flooded both and obliterated both – in the divine outer space of
    an owl

Ameen – in the thick woods hearing *Hu-Hu's* of that voice echoing clear –
Feathers tickling still along my tingling arms – ah the sweet embrace of an
    owl!

6/5

76   DEATH IN NEW YORK

I wonder when I die if my coffin will somehow end up in New York?
When I enter the company of the dead will I be invited to sup in New York?

What an odd thought – it came to me as I was doing *dhikr* after the prayer –
I thought of poets who've prophesied their deaths – *but drinking death's cup
    in New York?*

Death and New York have been closely wedded since September Eleventh –
A photo of towers collapsing and bodies falling doesn't need a blowup in
    New York

But I saw a blue coffin made of cardboard or cloud heading into the
    towering city –
A flash in the mind not surrounded by borders of buttercups in New York

You wonder where you'll die if you wonder at all – and no answer comes up –
It's just as possible the angel of death's given his thumbs up in New York!

A boat sloshes down Broadway or Madison Avenue or Times Square – it's
    the web-decked ship of death –
Ameen – this is probably all just a fantasy tempest in a teacup – in New York

6/6

77 DRUNK ON GOD'S NECTAR

The thirst for something almost intolerably sweet only gets stronger –
One sip from God's cup direct – one honey drop in the heart – and we
    crave something yet stronger

A thirsty wanderer comes to the backdoor of the outback – face and
    hands black – mouth crimson
The sun blazing behind him only makes his poignant silhouette stronger

The dry desert wasteland by the Egyptian Sphinx goes on forever –
That pitiless stare held sway for centuries – but now the minaret's
    stronger

The heart goes down a dark river in search of its fountaining source –
Each day that goes by wanting to be closer makes its true magnet stronger

If we broke through all at once and were drunk with love from now on
Would we have to say goodbye to all this knickknack world – where sad
    regret's stronger?

Drunk on pure nectar – aswim in pure nectar – will we ever reach shore?
Ameen – this life is long and full of scenes – but God's love's vignette's
    stronger!

6/6

78 APPLE PEEL EPIPHANY

I was peeling an apple in the sink round and round listening to a tape
    repeating the Name of God
When suddenly the peel went on forever extending past time and space
    as if ignited by the flame of God

Past walls and windows – out in the sky – past our planetary horizon
    completely –
The apple peel stretched way past even my own existence it seemed
    into the frame of God

It was only a moment – I don't mean to say it lasted as long as it seemed
But the peel went on spiraling under my knife as if in a whimsical game
    of God

Dizzy and bewildered for a second or two – holding the end of a mystical
    thread –
The peel uncoilingly reached into a mysterious dimension to the eternal
    acclaim of God

Mortal body in a material world – *Ameen* – things aren't at all what they
    seem –
Remembering God's true extra-spatial dimension seems to be a delightful
    aim of God!

6/7

JAVANESE GAMELAN MUSIC

What I love about Javanese gamelan music is how it seems to go past
     both ends endlessly –
It starts somewhere before the beginning and ends somewhere out past
     a rice field that bends endlessly

The soft chunking of metallophones as if down a celestial stairway –
     a musical slinky –
Has a way of grabbing the innermost heart that it then rends endlessly

A quavering voice floats weightlessly above the rhythmically structured
     tinkle
Echoing from far back in our collective memory that then extends
     endlessly

But with all this minute activity of voice and bell and flute and gong
Somehow this so-called primitive music brings time to a halt which it
     then suspends endlessly

As if on a long slow barge moving gradually through the stars –
The deliciously subtle stops and starts – clatter of sound in delicate collapse –
     it all ascends endlessly

The world's taken apart in this music – looked at through a prism
     – reassembled –
The drum heartbeat beats continuously – upon which it all depends
     endlessly

The music of these villagers and court musicians rises like a magic filigreed
    cloud –
Ameen – you're not alone on earth – these hearts and voices with a lover's
    soul that gloriously transcends endlessly

6/7

80 TIME TO SING

It's time to sing as only geese can sing – honking as they go across blue
  sky
Throw down your prayer carpet – light up your knees – let your heart's
  dhikr tattoo sky!

Throw open windows – lean way out – fling banners of God's praise –
Leap in the heart as if leaping up in a kangaroo sky!

Everything's drunk – *really!* walls – floors – inside – outside – everything
  that *is!*
Massive clouds move in brilliant herds – as if in a caribou sky!

Let nothing shut the love-heart in – let no shadow cross your breaths –
As if the earth weren't really earth but a wide-angled avenue sky!

Do you hear that sound – is it Rumi's flute – calling us back to the One?
A note held poignantly up in the stratosphere – God's true sky!

Sing – *Ameen* – let the heart stand up in your throat – let voices join with
  your voice!
Until finally the whole creation in one single voice can call *you* sky!

6/10

8 1　GLASS HOUSE IN CHINA

I passed a glass house on the way to China –
It was filled with glass vials on a tray in China

I entered the house to drink from my travels
For my thirst was intense that day in China

The vials were filled with a crystalline drink
Which I drank in one gulp – (that's the way in China)

The drink flowed deep and coursed through my veins
Then the world turned inside-out as if astray in China

Blue became yellow – red became green – white black
Everything a sweet fireworks display in China

At the center of it all shone a door of pure diamond –
Each facet extending its bright ray in China

I went through that door – and for an instant was not –
But when I continued on it was still day in China

Where had I been? – the world was more or less normal –
In this universe afloat in the Milky Way in China

I turned and the glass house was still there on its hill –
Trees were trees – streets streets – everything seemed
　　　　OK in China

I'd been stopped and died a death that was not quite
       physical
Since I didn't turn to dust or decay in China

O Mevlana – it wasn't China – *it was Konya all along* –
I have to say *ameen* – it's time to pray in China!

6/11

82 GOD'S MONOTONE

The rain's coming down outside my window – leaky pipes – a
    background monotone –
Raven the black cat on deep burgundy bedspread – green eyes
    blazing in pure round monotone –

The world's assembled in a cunning way to appear real to us –
If we saw it in its true dimensions we might feel a real profound
    monotone

What delight in a squirrel rooting for seeds among tall grasses –
Birds at the feeder trilling their variable compound monotone!

My heart wants to explode half the time and ignite into a sparkling
    flare –
Sometimes taking great self-control to keep it at an underground
    monotone

Gates of sparkling golden roses open at a single breath –
Especially if accompanied by the low heartbeat's homebound
    monotone

Underneath the surfaces of things and way behind appearances
A light shines against a screen of butterflies whose wings make a
    spellbound monotone

I sit at the feet of lions – *ameen* repeated over and over in their
    leonine purring –
And in the living roar of God's Majesty's long astounded monotone

6/16

83 TO SINK INTO SLEEP

To sink in sleep the way a mouse sinks into its hole – the way a violinist
      sinks into Beethoven's concerto – the way night sinks into day –
To wake when night is over – to rise like light from the sea floor – like a
      letter from God – like an eye that unblinks into day

Spreading arms I want to float above Byzantium – Rome – Constantinople
      and Konya – Enugu and Oakland where I was born –
Though the whole earth is our birthplace and we're getting reborn as each
      thought or anti-thought Tiddly Winks into day

Sitting under a cloud in the shape of the Tree of Life – each branch heavy
      with a different provincial ripe fruit –
I look up and see only God – Light streaming everywhere – as my heartbeat
      writes out God's Name on itself – in indelible inks on the day

Though imprisoned in a dream – in raincoat and hat – on the trail of a lost
      book – a lost soul – one thread left only –
All my paraphernalia of sleuthing – each eager supposition – rethinks into
      day

Light comes from everywhere – actions done or left undone – kindnesses –
      splendid urges – loving thoughts –
Ameen – human sieve for Allah – bathe in the light as its rays stream
      through God's invisible chinks into day

6/16

84 GORGEOUS IN SILVER BLUE RAIMENT

Gorgeous in silver blue raiment as it majestically passes before us –
It walks with rich and stately step slow as molasses before us

Hidden by the light of day as a prowling tiger is by leaves –
Naked as the moon by night with all the radiance it amasses before us

O my heart do you recognize its pace or its glint as it reveals its facets?
Do you openly embrace it by night as its soul trespasses before us?

Two hearts against each other beating in close syncopation –
That's how this love is – dazzling sunlight pouring into mountain
        crevasses before us

Don't hide in matter feeble one – don't cringe into the doings of the day –
When coat and clothes are removed the light's arranged in looking
        glasses before us

The ache's in not knowing always – our hearts are bereft without Him –
Listen to the music of His Voice in the pulse in your head as the world
        harasses before us

The moment is gone – a mockingbird sings in a tree – it's dawn – time
        to pray –
Ameen – worlds come and go – like so many multicolored vaporous
        gasses before us

6/19

85 AS I SIT AT THE TABLE

As I sit at a table my form dissolves almost completely away –
My hand holds a pen – my head's full of rapid bird-wings
        fanning fleetly away –

Hand holding pen – head full of birds – air-conditioning whirring –
Where am I? It seems my actual being is dissolving neatly away

Yet I am here – but I want Allah here – and me to be nowhere –
Is it in the fine-pointed ache of perception that notions like this won't
        go obsoletely away?

That if I am He is not – *if He is* I am not?
If only Allah exists in reality I should really tiptoe discreetly away –

But it's not quite like this I know – it's not a mental idea at all –
When a cow moos the moo hangs in the meadow's air while its
        moo-maker is hidden incompletely away –

I sit here puzzling this out – when in fact it's no puzzle at all –
Love – *burning love* – for Allah remains while you – *Ameen* – pass
        sweetly away

6/19

86 THE PROPHET MUHAMMAD WALKED IN

The Prophet Muhammad walked in – his face a moon – his head
      represented by God's flame
The room filled with rose-scent – the windows with doves – in our hearts we
      scented God's flame

How on earth did a man like this come among us? How beloved of Allah –
      how kind!
All who saw him as nothing but a mad relative became demented by God's
      flame

The world was reversed by him – inside became outside – outside became in –
Each word came from Truth's conflagration – descended by God's flame

It burned up this old world and replaced it with a pure one –
Both world and self entering purifying fire – even if resenting God's flame

His touch was sure – his tread so light – his smile creation's first morning
      on earth –
In his eyes was inexpressible perfection – augmented by God's flame

His voice pronounced words spaced like individual pearls on a string –
We hear them as clearly today – as though aged and fermented by God's
      flame

A star straight above him in the Unseen points him out wherever he goes –
Allah's increasing love for him through the centuries – as portended by
      God's flame

As the Prophet passes we long for him to stay – to turn to us – bathing in
      his light –
Allah's most beloved before anything was even invented by God's flame

His sweetheart – His intimate – His Messenger – His most cherished
      creation –
Just hearing his name pours new stars into the sky – supplemented by
      God's flame

In a dark smoky corner of the world – as far as China – as near as our
      jugular vein –
The pulse of the Divine throbs out his name – linked forever with God's –
      implemented by God's flame

This firmament – each lineament – each filament – each element –
Ameen – his graces flow without limit or measurement – documented by
      God's flame!

6/20

87 CATCH A RAINBOW

Catch a rainbow in its arc if you can – hold a sunbeam in your stilled
heart –
Run to the edge of the world and look out past its sad unfulfilled heart

Let love live in the words of your lip – let it flow like spiritual milk –
A mother makes herself available to all in her domiciled heart

Wheels flutter past like wings – wheels of bicycles and whirring minds –
Transparent walls and transparent people – don't let them give you a
chilled heart

See hawks wheeling! Over and over on circling updrafts and waves –
Invisible as the air the hawk floats along on – use your deftly skilled heart

I'm actually just talking to myself – it's quiet here and I'm all alone –
Raven the black cat at my left foot asleep – dreaming a happily mouse
killed heart

Canyons catch sunlight in silence – like glittering mirrors majestic in space –
Ameen – by extending inches of time and breath – God give me a constantly
thrilled heart!

6/21

88 OH ALLAH!

A tree in the woods beyond earshot of any cried *Oh Allah!*
Two bits of star debris in space began to collide – *Oh Allah!*

A groom pushed back the veil of his bride – *Oh Allah!*
A murderer paused for a crucial second to decide – *Oh Allah!*

The pupil of her master saw her heart open wide – *Oh Allah!*
A flying horse took her for a transcontinental ride – *Oh Allah!*

A young doctor kneeled by his first dark bedside – *Oh Allah!*
A baby opened its eyes for the first time but was cross-eyed – *Oh Allah!*

The goose at the head of the formation began to glide – *Oh Allah!*
The Prophet Muhammad is our most perfect guide – *Oh Allah!*

Bonnie for a moment took a long look at Clyde – *Oh Allah!*
Sacco and Vanzetti didn't quicken their stride – *Oh Allah!*

Orca the whale showed its enormous backside – *Oh Allah!*
The drowning sailor smiled and scrambled astride – *Oh Allah!*

Cells deep in the essence of matter began to divide – *Oh Allah!*
A world with its own slow solar system turns inside – *Oh Allah!*

A pirate ship with chests of rubies pulled alongside – *Oh Allah!*
Two mountaineers clung to the rocks of a mountainside – *Oh Allah!*

Ameen – this could go on – not only here but worldwide – *Oh Allah!*
But I'll stop – awed now and gratefully wide-eyed – *Oh Allah!*

6/22

89 WAKING UP

"Well at least I'm glad I'm still alive" – he said waking up –
"My body washed like one who's dead – but waking up!"

Back in the world of the ten thousand marvelous things
He saw light both inside and outside his head waking up

He flexed his two arms and felt how their hands wriggle –
He stretched his body full length on his bed – waking up

A hungry vulture wasn't wheeling in the sky above him –
He didn't even look particularly underfed – waking up

An enormous black butterfly landed right on his nose
And filled him with a certain existential dread – waking up

The world opened up like a gradual fan before him
All the way from China to the tip of his forehead – waking up

Where was he? In a back room? In an elephant's shadow?
He couldn't identify the source of his dread – waking up

He followed a light like a lamp in the air above a lagoon –
It floated above his in-and-out breath-thread – waking up

A thousand eyes in the air of every crisp living thing
As alive as he was (though perhaps not as thoroughbred) – waking up

"Let's go back to the mere fact" – he thought – *"of my awakening"* –
In spite of the world's temptations he couldn't be misled – waking up

"I could go to Madagascar – or walk through that door to Siam –
But I'm going to stand up right here where I am instead – waking up"

Like a dolphin loose in the sea – he found himself aswim in God's element
With God's light in every interstitial space – glass of milk – slice of bread –
      waking up

He opens his heart like the prayer of someone facing a sudden tidal wave –
Not closing clam-like but pouring out a sudden fountainhead waking up

The click of each moment a new world coming into view –
Each portion of our existence a body-shaped binocular into Godhead –
      waking up

He ends his prayer with *ameen* – turns for a moment from the Glory –
Keeping it deep within him – now he walks with lighter tread – waking up

6/24

THE RUMI INDUSTRY

There are those who dare not speak His Name –
Afraid their tongues (or hearts) will turn to flame?
They fabricate a "gossamer" world...

I've watched the Rumi video with Robert Bly – Coleman Barks
Deepak Chopra – Huston Smith – Debra Winger – *oh well...*

They've made it seem that Rumi – his spirit vast as sky –
Was just a divinely inspired *earthly* singer – *oh well...*

Fearing one fancy thing or another (none could mention God by Name)
Nor that Rumi – great Friend of Allah – was one of God's true
      message-bringers – *oh well*

They didn't seem to want to specify Rumi's subject as God *per se* –
But to keep it "open and flowing and human" – making Mevlana a kind of
      deeper New Age folksinger – *oh well*

Rumi was never afraid – *how could he be!* – heart a blazing light –
But they've made him into a kind of delirious bee with no stinger – *oh well*

Homogenize everything according to your comfort – grind everything more
      or less flat –
It cuts off the chance for total annihilation in Allah – for which Rumi
      was true bell-ringer – *oh well*

Rumi – passionate flame of love – moth and candle both – *sheer conflagration!*
But what do *you* know about it all *Ameen* – we're *all* finally put through God's nitty-gritty soul-wringer – *oh well!*

6/27

91 BRIGHT YELLOW HOUSE

A bright yellow house on a bright yellow hill turns into the flame of life –
Light beamed from heaven onto the tiniest creature gives it the name of
life

The throne room is empty – the courtiers are gone – the throne is alone –
The king – who's evaporated as well – asks *"Whatever became of life?"*

Three golden pebbles rattle at the bottom of a stream – bright water
rushing over –
"Are we only valuable if a gold miner finds us? In his frame of life?"

Passengers jump on – one by one – their baggage stowed – they sit—
Some sleep – some wake – some break through into heaven – on the train
of life

A little window opens up – a door slams – a road widens – a handle appears –
Faces quizzical – hearts bewildered – answers come and go in the game of
life

Dame Self and Master Ego berate each other constantly – neither wins –
The soul is worn to battling tatters and flapping shreds – in the crying
shame of life

Ameen – you didn't even mean to begin this poem – you sat down and
out it came –
Things have a way of proclaiming themselves – then you simply declaim in
life…

6/28

92 IMMORTAL

We're mortal while we're alive – and when we die we become immortal –
If we dream we wake up while dreaming we know what it is to die – and
    become immortal

We move along a track of living light without a break –
Entering the tavern with friends but leaving it as a lonesome immortal

I lift the glass in the air and moonlight streams through it!
Allah so kind in this jeweled paradise of earth – even our bizarre cerebellum –
    immortal!

Egrets of mist might fly out of our eyes into the clouds –
Imps of delight might do cartwheels around our legs – *frolicsome immortals!*

We die – that's for sure – body collapsing gradually or all at once in great
    folds like a circus tent –
But we can hear our heartbeats already striding out – their brave kettledrum –
    immortal!

Inside each pulse a grateful thought pillowed by angels –
Carried beyond this earth's inevitable martyrdom – *immortal!*

Exchanging one dome of stars for another – other lights – other
    constellations –
We glide along even now surrounded by its vast transparent stadium –
    immortal!

Our eyes close in sleep or death – the world opens like a treasure cave of
   lights –
Love of Allah takes us directly to Him – in a sweet delirium – *immortal!*

Ameen as our lips are sealed – *Ameen* as the world shuts down for good –
Ameen – as fingers play a celestial harmonium – *immortal!*

6/29

ACKNOWLEDGMENTS ALL AROUND

I have to thank my bones all these many years for just being there for me!
Thank you's in order from femurs to metatarsal – none the worse for wear –
 for me!

Thanks due also to the major and lesser organs – tucked invisibly away –
For reliable inner workings there's simply none to compare – for me

Turning food to fuel — acids chomping away so heartily – a second feast!
And the fact they do it so efficiently – and all without silverware! – for me

I'd like to acknowledge as well my respiratory passages – *well done!*
Keeping ducts open from big to those hair-thin capillaries – with no grand
 fanfare – for me!

It makes breathing a lot easier by just generally being so porous –
Letting oxygen spread throughout the bodily system with a certain *savoir
 faire* – for me

Thanks also to the eyes – magical orbs – soul mirrors – taking things in so
 prettily –
And the wonderful fact that they come in a stereoscopic pair – for me

Dear brain – wherever you are – in skull – yes – but behind so much!
Without you I don't know what I'd do – I swear – for me

And the castle and the road to the castle and the weather at the castle –
 usually so fair!
The heart! Twenty-four-seven – keeping a jazzy rhythm – your sovereignty
 I declare – for me

And yet all of these together owe all their concerted togetherness to One
    only – *Allah!*
Behind everything He's the bankrolling trillion – nay – *gazillionaire* – for
    me

So thanks to God and His physical minions this dawn just before prayer
As I sit – *Ameen* – writing this ghazal on the side of my bed in my long
    underwear – for me

7/2

94 FACE OF DEATH

The face of death's almost like the face of life –
But stone mask of wrinkles and frozen eyes takes the place of life

In old age – just before death – the senses gallop away –
Wild horses stampeding from the limited body's space of life

A stick in the desert casts lengthening and shortening shadows –
Sunlight filters down through whatever stands as the lace of life

A smile flickering across the face may be all that's left –
After a lifetime of expressions it may be the ultimate trace of life

Can't a giant orb of light – God's heavenly dimension – take over?
Can't His exalted height of divinity overcome the disgrace of life?

We move inexorably through mortality's door – *may it grow light!*
May we increase in wisdom's enlightened stature as we leave the
       embrace of life!

This hope – this promise – this prophetic expectation – this joy!
It's all you have – *Ameen* – as you praise the unending grace of life

7/11

95 HOLE IN SPACE

It's a hole in space we rise into as if lifting a torch!
Our own particular hole in space uplifting a torch!

You're there or you're not there – mask on or off –
What wind blows – what reality – shape-shifting a torch!

I left your invitation on the boardwalk fluttering behind me –
Whitecaps rise all around it – as if handkerchiefing a torch

Has a crime been committed – its perpetrator passing on?
Has he come and gone – like an arsonist sniffing a torch?

This universe holds our lives for a moment – hearts afire with longing –
We don't often know what for – as if on a current simply drifting a torch –

Let's take what we're given – *Ameen* – to here from the Unseen!
We've been given a light to see Allah by – as if He's *gifting* a torch!

7/12

96 TINY ELFIN BEINGS

Tiny elfin beings in pointed green hats inhabit the flame of love –
It spreads like ink on water – like light on a lake – as we exclaim our love

Edges disappear inside the assorted things of this world
Until nothing at all exits outside the frame of love

She enters in white holding the moon like a shimmering shield –
He enters stage left with the sun like a bow taking aim at love

Has the world gone mad at last – all of it even down to its spiders?
Hate malice and violence – and everyone wants to put the blame on love!

Gather up pearls and rubies scattered on the roadways – *Ameen* –
String them again and place them around our hearts in order to reclaim our
    love

What's the point of living if we die screaming like frozen mummies?
No! – we need to be those whose hearts are always ready to proclaim our
    love

7/13

97 SINGING

An angel sits on a flowing silver rock by a slow waterfall singing –
A face in the clouds lights up brighter than an ignited snowball singing

A line of animals up a steep green hill seems to extend throughout time –
Nothing alive stays motionless – everything urges on to answer the divine
     call singing

Molecules and atoms in their galactic orbits shed radiant light –
Turning in Majesty's gaze – even if they merely crawl – singing

Releasing a million birds into the sky – a million turquoise fish in the sea –
You wonder how Allah every moment has the endless wherewithal –
     singing!

I'm a great sinner – no doubt about it – as pure as flood muck –
I open my mouth to praise and it comes out a cracked caterwaul – singing

This dark universe can't trap us – it turns its black curtains around –
Where there was drought and despair now there's God's compassionate
     rainfall – singing

Hope in my heart – like a single bead of light – with the universe inside –
Ameen – take another drink of light's ecstatic alcohol – *singing!*

7/19

98   ONE DAY DEATH KNOCKED

One day death knocked and knocked and no one answered –
Only the door's wood-grain in resounding unison answered

A water drop on the lip of a glass was held suspended –
Only shadows cast by trees like oars on a galleon answered

We were all safely dead to death – we were all satisfied –
Not even the xylophone bones of one skeleton answered

Death was stymied – death turned livid – not used to this treatment –
We'd reached a state of eternal life – as if only a jaunty disembodied
          accordion answered

But it may have only lasted an eternal nanosecond –
Because finally – after a non-temporal millennium or two – someone
          answered

The door swung open – now we were face to face with death again –
And all of us who by then had been by life undone – answered

But it was a different answer – it was a smile of sweet recognition alone –
It was an easy flow in which we – held in love's burning sun – answered

The knock comes – in the middle of the night or morning – always
          uniquely –
But we can't leave the knock – for all its intrusion – undone –
          unanswered

The whole universe resounds with its tapping – its light fist on our door –
But like a spy on this side of the door – death's work must be well done –
answered!

Ameen – breathing easily in your chair by the window and its clustering
birds –
When death knocks may you always remember to respond to none but the
One – and answer!

7/21

99   LAST SHOOTOUT

Life takes out its six-guns and shoots toward glorious death –
Its desperado bullets fly faster and faster through time to a notorious
      death

As bullets fly the gap gets shorter and shorter between them and death –
But it's life who does all the work here zeroing in on laborious death

Life's all dressed up – the eternally romantic lover in costly linens and silks –
To woo ever more closer and more intimate shy but desperately amatorious
      death

Those silver bullets of his fly faster than a tightrope walker
Who fearing a fall starts running on his rope away from a vainglorious death

Or a clown who rides a pony festooned with bells – does somersaults –
Hoping to elude the dark visage of tragedy and fly into an uproarious death

Or one who hangs upside-down – sloth-like – from long forest branches
      asleep
Hoping to be passed over – forgetting the fact of an arboreous death

But life – in boots and ten gallon hat – strides ever forward
Hoping in the last shootout to be granted at least a victorious death

Or then there's the one who – filled with the vast Light of Allah –
Drops the old garment and floats forward to a sparklingly euphorious death

Not like the head executioner – severe in black leather hood –
Who chops from a great height the sharp blade of an inquisitorious
  death

Or even the bland egg-shaped person never fully come to life
Who may opt for a neatly purgatorious or mildly meritorious death

But rather one who sheds gun and holster altogether – and stands raw
  as rain –
Blending into the storm and flash of a sublimely *thunderorious* death

Whatever – *Ameen* – now sixty-two – dreaming in health and peace and
  expectation –
To be one day released from this world's prison – to a *whatever's in-store-
  for-us* – death

8/2

ABOUT THE AUTHOR

Born in 1940 in Oakland, California, Daniel Abdal-Hayy Moore's first book of poems, *Dawn Visions*, was published by Lawrence Ferlinghetti of City Lights Books, San Francisco, in 1964, and the second in 1972, *Burnt Heart/Ode to the War Dead*. He created and directed *The Floating Lotus Magic Opera Company* in Berkeley, California in the late 60s, and presented two major productions, *The Walls Are Running Blood*, and *Bliss Apocalypse*. He became a Sufi Muslim in 1970, performed the Hajj in 1972, and lived and traveled throughout Morocco, Spain, Algeria and Nigeria, landing in California and publishing *The Desert is the Only Way Out*, and *Chronicles of Akhira* in the early 80s (Zilzal Press). Residing in Philadelphia since 1990, in 1996 he published *The Ramadan Sonnets* (Jusoor/City Lights), and in 2002, *The Blind Beekeeper* (Jusoor/Syracuse University Press). He has been the major editor for a number of works, including *The Burdah* of Shaykh Busiri, translated by Shaykh Hamza Yusuf, and the poetry of Palestinian poet, Mahmoud Darwish, translated by Munir Akash. He is also widely published on the worldwide web: *The American Muslim*, *DeenPort*, and his own website, among others: www.danielmoorepoetry.com. The Ecstatic Exchange Series is bringing out the extensive body of his works of poetry, beginning in 2005 with *Mars & Beyond, Laughing Buddha Weeping Sufi, Salt Prayers* and a revised edition of *Ramadan Sonnets*, and continuing in 2006 beginning with *Psalms for the Brokenhearted, I Imagine a Lion, Coattails of the Saint, Love is a Letter Burning in a High Wind* and *Abdallah Jones and the Disappearing-Dust Caper*. *The Flame of Transformation Turns to Light* is the first volume in 2007, with further publications if God wills.

POETIC WORKS BY DANIEL ABDAL-HAYY MOORE

Published and Unpublished
(many to appear in *The Ecstatic Exchange* Series)

Dawn Visions (published by City Lights, 1964)
Burnt Heart/Ode to the War Dead (published by City Lights, 1972)
This Body of Black Light Gone Through the Diamond (printed by Fred Stone, Cambridge, Mass, 1965)
On The Streets at Night Alone (1965?)
All Hail the Surgical Lamp (1967)
States of Amazement (1970)

Abdullah Jones and the Disappearing-Dust Caper (published by The Ecstatic Exchange, Crescent Series, 2006)
The Chronicles of Akhira (1981) (published by Zilzal Press with Typoglyphs by Karl Kempton, 1986)
Mouloud (1984) (A Zilzal Press chapbook, 1995)
Man is the Crown of Creation (1984)
The Look of the Lion (The Parabolas of Sight) (1984)
The Desert is the Only Way Out (completed 4/21/84) (Zilzal Press chapbook, 1985)
Atomic Dance (1984) (am here books, 1988)
Outlandish Tales (1984)
Awake as Never Before (12/26/84) (Zilzal Press chapbook, 1993)
Glorious Intervals (1/1/85) (Zilzal Press chapbook, ?)
Long Days on Earth/Book I (1/28 – 8/30/85)
Long Days on Earth/Book II (Hayy Ibn Yaqzan)
Long Days on Earth/Book III (1/22/86)
Long Days on Earth/Book IV (1986)
The Ramadan Sonnets (Long Days on Earth/Book V) (5/9 – 6/11/86) (Published by Jusoor/ City Lights Books, 1996) (Republished as **Ramadan Sonnets** by The Ecstatic Exchange 2005)
Long Days on Earth/Book VI (6-8/30/86)
Holograms (9/4/86 – 3/26/87)
History of the World (The Epic of Man's Survival) (4/7 – 6/18/87)
Exploratory Odes (6/25 – 10/18/87)
The Man at the End of the World (11/11 – 12/10/87)
The Perfect Orchestra (3/30 – 7/25/88)
Fed from Underground Springs (7/30 – 11/23/88)
Ideas of the Heart (11/27/88 – 5/5/89)
New Poems (scattered poems, out of series, from 3/24 – 8/9/89)
Facing Mecca (5/16 – 11/11/89)
A Maddening Disregard for the Passage of Time (11/17/89 – 5/20/90)

The Heart Falls in Love with Visions of Perfection (6/15/90 – 6/2/91)

Like When You Wave at a Train and the Train Hoots Back at You (Farid's Book) (6/11 –
7/26/91)

Orpheus Meets Morpheus (8/1/91– 3/14/92)

The Puzzle (3/21/92 – 8/17/93)

The Greater Vehicle (10/17/93 – 4/30/94)

A Hundred Little 3-D Pictures (5/14/94 – 9/11/95)

The Angel Broadcast (9/29 – 12/17/95)

Mecca/Medina Time-Warp (12/19/95 – 1/6/96) (Published as a Zilzal Press chapbook, 1996)

Miracle Songs for the Millennium (1/20 – 10/16/96)

The Blind Beekeeper (11/15/96 – 5/30/97) (Published 2002 by Jusoor/Syracuse University
Press)

Chants for the Beauty Feast (6/3 – 10/28/97)

Open Doors (10/29/97 – 5/23/98)

Salt Prayers (5/29 – 10/24/98) (Published by The Ecstatic Exchange, 2005)

Some (10/25/98 – 4/25/99)

Flight to Egypt (5/1 – 5/16/99)

I Imagine a Lion (5/21 – 11/15/99) (Published by The Ecstatic Exchange, 2006)

Millennial Prognostications (11/25/99 – 2/2/2000)

The Book of Infinite Beauty (2/4 – 10/8/2000)

Blood Songs (10/9/2000 – 4/3/2001)

The Music Space (4/10 – 9/16/2001)

Where Death Goes (9/20/2001 – 5/1/2002)

The Flame of Transformation Turns to Light (99 Ghazals Written in English) (5/14 – 8/21/
2002) (Published by The Ecstatic Exchange, 2007)

Through Rose-Colored Glasses (7/22/2002 – 1/15/2003)

Psalms for the Broken-Hearted (1/22 – 5/25/2003) (Published by The Ecstatic Exchange,
2006)

Hoopoe's Argument (5/27 – 9/18/03)

Love is a Letter Burning in a High Wind (9/21 – 11/6/2003) (Published by The Ecstatic
Exchange, 2006)

Laughing Buddha/Weeping Sufi (11/7/2003 – 1/10/2004) (Published by The Ecstatic
Exchange, 2005)

Mars and Beyond (1/20 – 3/29/2004) (Published by The Ecstatic Exchange, 2005)

Underwater Galaxies (4/5 – 7/21/2004)

Cooked Oranges (7/23/2004 – 1/24/2005

Holiday from the Perfect Crime (1/25 – 6/11/2005)

Stories Too Fiery to Sing Too Watery to Whisper (6/13 – 10/24/2005)

Coattails of the Saint (10/26/2005 – 5/10/2006) (Published by The Ecstatic Exchange, 2006)

In the Realm of Neither (5/14/2006 – 11/12/06)

Invention of the Wheel (11/13/06 –)

www.ingramcontent.com/pod-product-compliance
Lightning Source LLC
Chambersburg PA
CBHW030006110426
42736CB00040BA/517